FAIRY T·A·L·E·S

in

CROSS STITCH

FAIRY
T·A·L·E·S

in
CROSS STITCH

Dorothea Hall

MEREHURST

ACKNOWLEDGEMENTS

I would like to offer my special thanks to Alexander Hall for his assistance with the text of the fairy tales.

My grateful thanks are also due to the following people who helped with the cross stitching of the projects in this book with such skill and enthusiasm: Gisela Banbury, Clarice Blakey, Caroline Davies, Christina Eustace, Janet Grey and Anne Whitbourn.

Published 1992 by Merehurst Limited
Ferry House, 51-57 Lacy Road, Putney, London SW15 1PR

© Copyright 1992 Merehurst Limited
ISBN 1 85391 163 1 (Cased)
ISBN 1 85391 244 1 (Paperback)

A catalogue record for this book is available from the British Library.

Project Editor: Polly Boyd
Edited by Diana Brinton
Designed by Maggie Aldred
Photography by Di Lewis
Illustrations by John Hutchinson
Typesetting by Maron Graphics Limited
Colour separation by Fotographics Limited, London – Hong Kong
Printed in Italy by New Interlitho, S.p.A., Milan

Merehurst is the leading publisher of craft books and has an excellent range of titles to suit all levels. Please send to the address above for our free catalogue, stating the title of this book.

CONTENTS

ℐNTRODUCTION

In an age of increasing sophistication, it is heartening to see a revival of interest in traditional pastimes and to look back at the time when both needlework skills and story telling were passed on through the family, not by books and television, as so much is today, but by example and by word of mouth – in the nursery and sitting around the fireside over many long winter evenings.

It is not surprising that fairy tales have long been a constant and wonderful source of inspiration for a variety of artistic expressions. These include the seaside Punch and Judy show, childrens' cartoon films and the ever-popular Christmas pantomime where, even today, Puss in Boots, Cinderella or Old Mother Goose, for example, deliver a highly moral tale, usually in a fictional setting and full of knockabout humour. There is no doubt that these are some of the most famous stories of all time, whose special magic keeps children and adults alike spellbound, and happily enthralled for hours.

Over the years, fairy tales have been collected from different parts of the world by such well-known story tellers as Charles Perrault, Hans Andersen and the brothers Grimm, and have been illustrated with a zest and vitality that has often resulted in beautifully imaginative images. Indeed, so strongly do these images impress us as children that they remain with us for life.

In designing projects for the book, it has been my aim throughout to show the immense range of fairy tale images that are available, and to use as many as it was possible to translate into cross stitch motifs; motifs that would enhance relatively small projects and appeal to today's readers.

As the book contains instructions for more than thirty projects, space does not allow for descriptions of the permutations and alternative combinations that are possible. However, with a little skill and dexterity, you will be able to apply a design given in the book to a project of your choice. For example, instead of working the Gingerbread Man tablecloth you may prefer to work a single design for a nursery picture, perhaps adding a child's name and birth date (see the alphabet and numbers given at the back of the book). Alternatively, you could embroider all six designs and stitch them in sequence to make a toddler's washable picture book, or a nursery wall hanging, or use them for a quilt top – the possibilities are endless!

After encouraging the reader to be flexible with ideas, I should point out that before you decide to interchange designs and projects within the book, it is important to check first that the thread count is the same on both recommended fabrics, otherwise you will end up with a larger or smaller design. Whatever you decide to make, I hope that you will derive as much fun and enjoyment as I have had in researching and designing for the book.

If, on the other hand, you have never cross stitched before – and I know children love to try – a couple of border exercises or an initial (given at the back of the book) would be a good starting point. In this way, you would not only be learning a new craft skill, which you too may pass on eventually, but you would be making your own small sampler, one that will introduce you to a whole new world of creativity.

BEFORE YOU BEGIN

Each project begins with a full list of the materials that you will require, giving the precise measurements of fabrics, cardboard, trims and so on. Note that the measurements given for the embroidery fabric include a minimum of 3cm (1¼in) all around to allow for stretching it in a frame and preparing the edges to prevent them from fraying.

A colour key for DMC stranded embroidery cotton is given with each chart. It is assumed that you will need to buy one skein of each colour mentioned, even though you may use less, but where two or more skeins are needed, this information is included in the main list of requirements.

Should you wish to use Coats/Anchor, or Madeira, stranded embroidery cottons, refer to the conversion chart given at the back of the book (pages 126-127).

To work from the charts, particularly those where several symbols are used in close proximity, some readers may find it helpful to have the chart enlarged so that the squares and symbols can be seen more easily. Many photo-copying services will do this for a minimum charge.

When you begin to cross stitch, use the centre lines given on the chart and the basting threads on your fabric as reference points for counting the squares and threads to position your design accurately.

To help in making up the projects, references are made either to the Basic Skills section or to a project in the book, where a full explanation is given for the particular technique required.

FRINGED TABLECLOTH AND NAPKINS

Give your guests a special treat with this beautifully embroidered set of tablecloth and napkins. Their jolly motifs tell the story of the run-away gingerbread man and his ill-fated journey across the river.

◆◆◆

THE GINGERBREAD MAN

Thinking he is very clever, the newly-baked gingerbread man runs away over the fields, passing cows and horses, until he reaches a river and a wily old fox. Not wishing to miss an opportunity, the fox gives the little biscuit man a lift and, swimming lower in the water, suggests that he hops on his head, whereupon he opens his mouth and the biscuit man falls in!

FRINGED TABLECLOTH AND NAPKINS

YOU WILL NEED

For a tablecloth measuring 107cm (42in)
square, and four napkins measuring
41cm (16½in) square:

*190cm (2⅛yd) of pale blue evenweave
(Aida) fabric, 110cm (43in) wide, 16 threads
to 2.5cm (1in)
DMC stranded embroidery cotton in the colours
given in the panels shown on pages 14-18
4 skeins of DMC pale blue 800 for the hemstitching;
5 skeins of red 900 and 3 of ochre 782
No24 tapestry needle*

•

PREPARING THE FABRIC

Begin by removing the selvedges, cutting straight
along the grain of the fabric. Next, steam press the
fabric to remove all creases. Following the cutting
layout, cut out the tablecloth and napkins.

A 5cm (2in) allowance is included on all sides
of the tablecloth for the fringe, and 2.5cm (1in) on
the napkins. On each section, mark the depth of
the fringe with basting stitches: 5cm (2in) all
around on the tablecloth and 2.5cm (1in) all
around on the four napkins. Following the diagram
given opposite, baste the positioning lines (A,B,C,
D,E,F) for the cross stitch motifs as shown.

THE EMBROIDERY

Working in a hoop (see page 120) and following
the charts and colour keys given, complete the
embroidery, using two strands of thread in the
needle throughout. You will find it easier to work
all the cross stitching and then finish with the
backstitching on top.

As you move your hoop along from one motif to
another, try to avoid trapping motifs that have
already been stitched under the rings of the hoop.
A piece of tissue paper placed between the fabric
and hoop will help to prevent the embroidery from
becoming marked (see page 121).

Following the instructions given on page 124,
hemstitch around the edges, using three strands of
thread in the needle and working over two threads
for each stitch. Finally, remove the fabric threads
to make the fringing. Take out all the basting
stitches and steam press the finished cloth and
napkins on the wrong side.

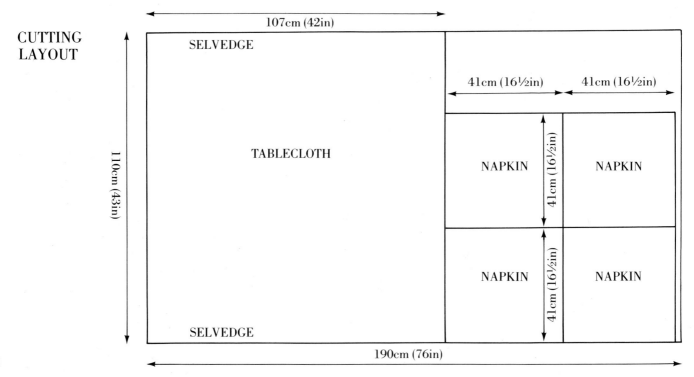

CUTTING
LAYOUT

107cm (42in)

SELVEDGE

41cm (16½in)   41cm (16½in)

110cm (43in)

TABLECLOTH

NAPKIN   41cm (16½in)   NAPKIN

NAPKIN   41cm (16½in)   NAPKIN

SELVEDGE

190cm (76in)

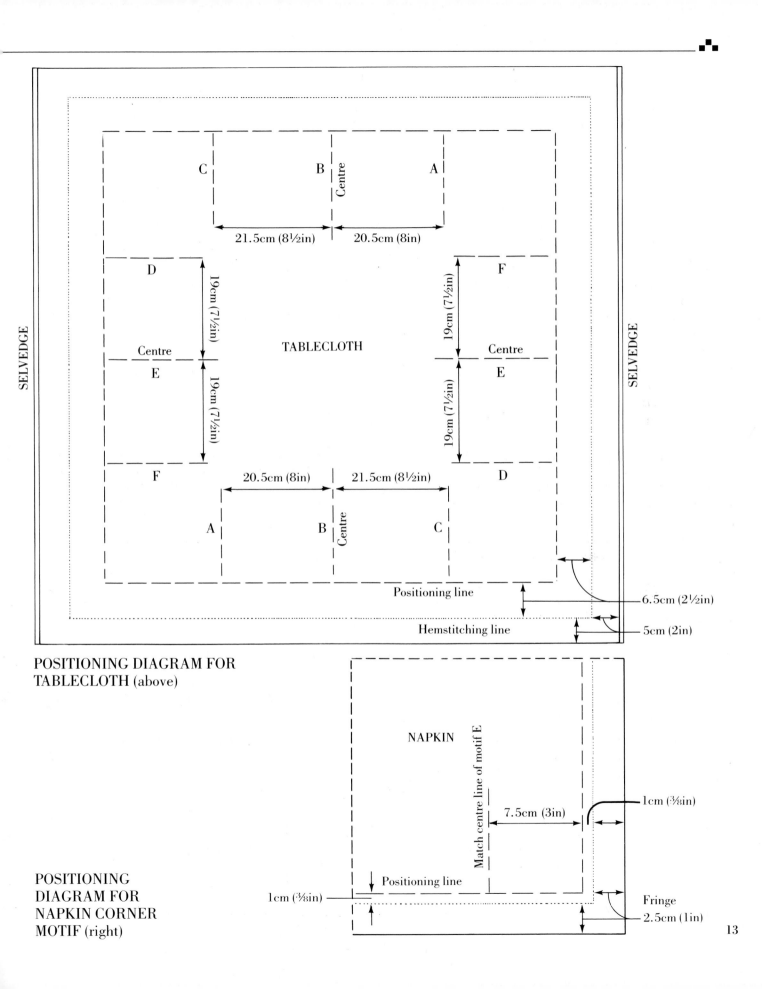

SELVEDGE

SELVEDGE

C   B   A

Centre

21.5cm (8½in)   20.5cm (8in)

D

19cm (7½in)

F

19cm (7½in)

Centre

Centre

TABLECLOTH

E

E

19cm (7½in)

19cm (7½in)

F   D

20.5cm (8in)   21.5cm (8½in)

A   B   C

Centre

Positioning line

6.5cm (2½in)

Hemstitching line

5cm (2in)

**POSITIONING DIAGRAM FOR
TABLECLOTH (above)**

NAPKIN

Match centre line of motif E

7.5cm (3in)

1cm (⅜in)

Positioning line

1cm (⅜in)

Fringe

2.5cm (1in)

**POSITIONING
DIAGRAM FOR
NAPKIN CORNER
MOTIF (right)**

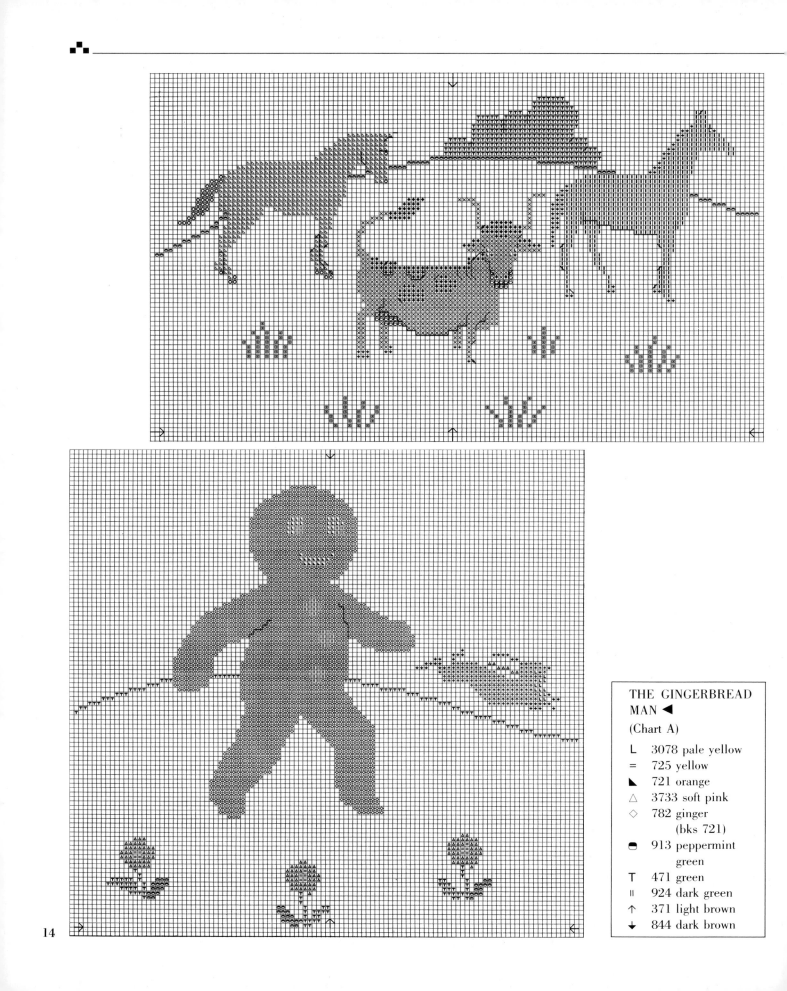

THE GINGERBREAD
MAN ◄

(Chart A)

L   3078 pale yellow

=   725 yellow

◣   721 orange

△   3733 soft pink

◇   782 ginger
     (bks 721)

⬭   913 peppermint
     green

T   471 green

‖   924 dark green

↑   371 light brown

↓   844 dark brown

◀ COWS AND HORSES
(Chart B)

L	3078	pale yellow
✕	738	corn (bks 680)
◆	680	deep gold
6	722	pink
⊡	3348	pale green
T	471	green
⊖	913	peppermint green
I	840	brown (bks 844)
↓	844	dark brown
◺	318	light grey (bks 317)
○	317	grey

THE FOX ▼
(Chart C)

L	3078	pale yellow
△	3733	soft pink
S	352	pink
✱	919	russet red (bks hairs on tail)
÷	900	red (bks 919)
A	799	blue
●	798	deep blue
	3348	pale green (bks far bank and grass)
T	471	green (bks grass)
H	3774	beige (bks mouth 844; bks throat 900)
↓	844	dark brown

GINGERBREAD MAN ON FOX'S TAIL ▲
(Chart D)

L	3078 pale yellow
◣	721 orange
△	3733 soft pink
⊑	352 coral pink
✱	919 russet red
◇	782 ginger (bks 721)
÷	900 red (bks around fox's mouth; bks 844)
‖	924 dark green
A	799 blue
●	798 dark blue (bks water)
H	3774 beige
↓	844 dark brown

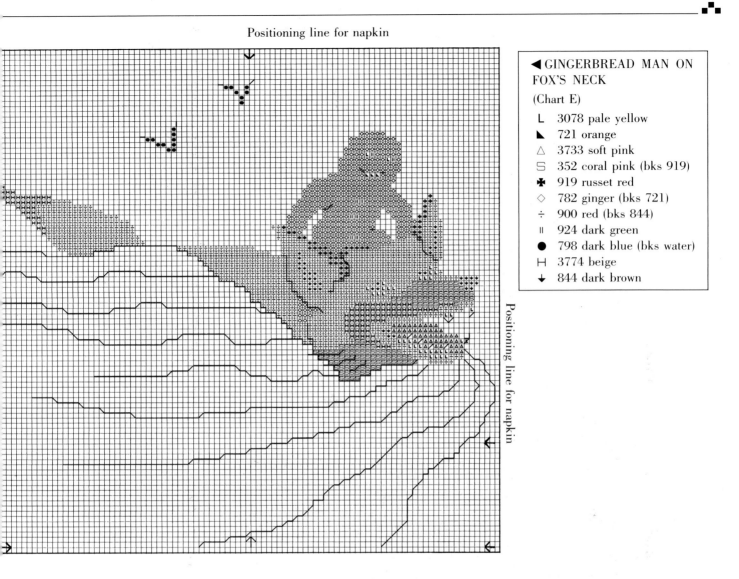

Positioning line for napkin

◀ GINGERBREAD MAN ON
FOX'S NECK

(Chart E)

L 3078 pale yellow
◣ 721 orange
△ 3733 soft pink
S 352 coral pink (bks 919)
✱ 919 russet red
◇ 782 ginger (bks 721)
÷ 900 red (bks 844)
‖ 924 dark green
● 798 dark blue (bks water)
H 3774 beige
↓ 844 dark brown

ALTERNATIVE GROUND FABRICS

Granted that natural linens and even wide cotton evenweaves can be relatively expensive to purchase, you may find that you already possess a suitable plain tablecloth and napkins which you would prefer to embroider. These will almost certainly not be made from an evenweave fabric, but fortunately, provided that the fabric is plain and has a smooth surface, it is possible to embroider it with a cross stitch design by working through a fine needlepoint canvas, basted in position on the fabric.

You must use canvas with a mesh size that matches that of the evenweave for which the design is intended. For example, for the Gingerbread Man design, you should choose a 16 count canvas.

Begin by cutting a piece of canvas for each motif that you wish to cross stitch, cutting the canvas slightly larger than the motif. Following the instructions given with positioning layout, baste any positioning lines on the canvas and than baste the canvas in position on the ground fabric, covering the area that is to be embroidered. Align the threads of the canvas with the grain of the fabric.

Following the colour key, stitch through the canvas and the ground fabric, treating the canvas as the evenweave and making sure that the cross stitching does not pierce the canvas threads.

Complete the cross stitching; remove the basting stitches, and then – one by one – withdraw the canvas threads, easing them carefully out from the embroidery. Finish by embroidering the backstitch details on top.

Steam press on the wrong side, in the usual way.

GINGERBREAD MAN ABOUT
TO BE EATEN ▲

(Chart F)

L   3078 pale yellow
▶   721 orange
△   3733 soft pink
S   352 coral pink (bks 900)
✳   919 russet red
◇   782 ginger (bks 721)
÷   900 red (bks 844; bks
    hairs on neck 900)
▣   3348 pale green

        913 peppermint green
            (bks near grass)
T   471 green
‖   924 dark green
A   799 blue
    798 dark blue
        (bks water and birds)
H   3774 beige
↓   844 dark brown

TEA-COSY

Embroidered in bright, cheery colours, this large, padded cosy will keep your tea steaming hot right to the last cup.

HANSEL AND GRETEL

Having been abandoned deep in the woods, Hansel and Gretel fell fast asleep. When they awoke it was dusk and Gretel began to cry, 'How shall we get out of the wood?' Hansel comforted her saying, 'Wait until the moon rises, and then we'll quickly find the way.'

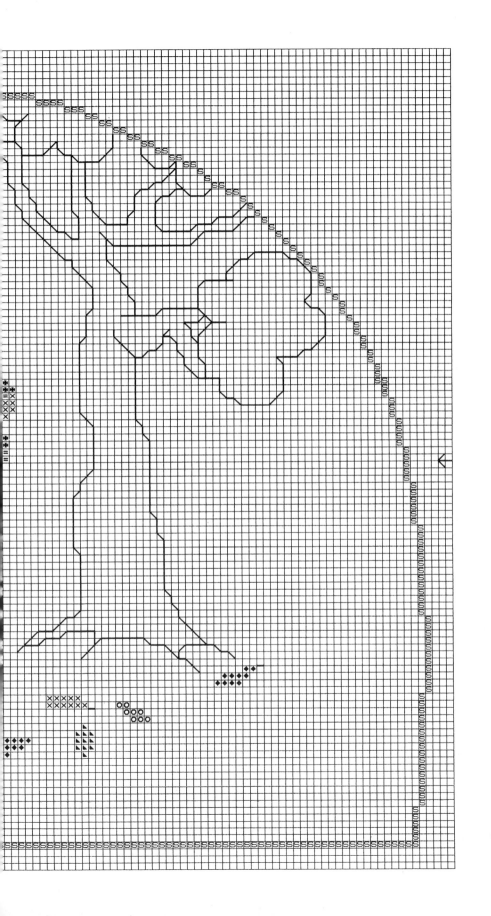

◄ HANSEL AND GRETEL

◇   white (bks 799)

✕   743 pale yellow (bks 833)

=   972 yellow

○   833 deep gold (bks on right
tree – second to top cluster
of leaves; left tree – second
to bottom cluster of leaves)

÷   951 flesh (bks 869)

✱   224 pink

| 223 rose pink

◆   976 ginger (bks on right tree –
top and bottom clusters of
leaves; left tree – second to
top and bottom clusters
of leaves)

●   900 red (bks on right tree –
smallest cluster of leaves;
left tree – top cluster
of leaves)

S   732 green

◣   733 olive green (bks tree
trunks and branches)

◗   747 pale turquoise

‖   597 turquoise (bks 733)

◩   799 blue

✦   3750 dark blue (bks 799)

⊡   3799 very dark blue

△   869 brown
(bks bird's eye and legs)

TEA-COSY

For a tea-cosy measuring 37cm × 27cm
(14½in × 10½in):

90cm × 30cm (36in × 12in) of blue evenweave
Lugana, 26 threads to 2.5 cm (1in)
90cm × 60cm (36in × 24in) of pale blue lawn
for the lining
76cm × 30cm (30in × 12in) of medium-weight
synthetic batting
150cm (60in) of red bias binding, 2.5cm (1in) wide
DMC stranded embroidery cotton in the colours
given in the panel on page 20
No 24 tapestry needle
Matching sewing threads
Tracing paper

•

THE EMBROIDERY

Cut the evenweave fabric in half to give two pieces, each measuring 45cm × 30cm (18in × 12in). With the edges of one section prepared and stretched in a hoop, baste the positioning lines for the embroidery, as shown on the chart.

Complete the embroidery, using two strands of thread throughout, except for the outlines around both faces and hands, where a single thread is used. Steam press the finished embroidery on the wrong side.

MAKING UP THE TEA-COSY

To make the paper pattern for the cosy, first enlarge the graph pattern given opposite on tracing paper (see page 122), and cut out. Seam allowances of 12mm (½in) all around are included.

Place the pattern on the evenweave fabric with straight grain and centre lines matching, and cut out. In the same way, cut out the lining and the batting as instructed.

To facilitate laundering, the outer cover of the cosy is detachable from the lining and is simply bound around the edges with bias binding.

For the loop, cut 8cm (3in) of contrast bias bind-ing and machine stitch the long edges together.

Fold in half to form a loop. Baste to the centre top of the front section, laying it on the right side of the fabric, raw edges placed just inside the seam allowance.

With right sides outside, place both sections of the cosy together and baste around the curved edge. Pin and baste the double-folded bias binding around the curved edge and machine stitch, using matching sewing thread. Trim the binding level with the lower edge. Bind the lower edge in the same way, overlapping the cut ends by 12mm (½in). Cut the end with the grain of the bias and fold under 6mm (¼in) to neaten. Remove all basting stitches and press the finished cover.

THE LINING

Place the four lining sections in two pairs, each with right sides together, and baste and stitch the bottom edges, taking 12mm (½in) seams. Press the seams and turn each section right side out.

Cut 12mm (½in) from the bottom edge of each batting section, and pin a batting section into each lining pocket. Baste along the curved seamline, then place the two lining sections together and machine zigzag along the curved seam. Trim the excess fabric, close to the stitching, and slip the lining inside the cover to complete the tea-cosy.

TEA COSY

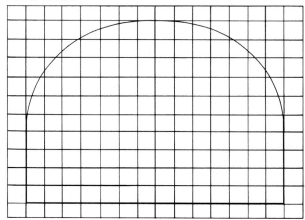

1 SQUARE = 2.5cm (1in)
Cut two from evenweave
Cut two from batting
Cut four from lining

TEA-POT STAND

To protect your table from
unsightly stains, here is a
glass-topped tea-pot stand to
accompany the tea cosy on
page 19.

THE DONKEY WHO
FETCHED THE SEA

Far away in the Arabian desert, Chaki the
donkey heard that the only well in the village
where he lived had completely dried up.
Thinking he must do something to help but
not sure which direction to take, he set off
saying, 'I'll go and find the sea and bring it
back to the village.'

TEA-POT STAND

YOU WILL NEED

For a hexagonal tea-pot stand measuring
18cm (7¼in) overall, with a 13cm (5in)
circular centre:

*20cm (8in) square of blue Aida fabric,
14 threads to 2.5cm (1in)
DMC stranded embroidery cotton in the colours
given in the panel
No 26 tapestry needle
Hexagonal tea-pot stand
(for suppliers, see page 128)*

•

THE EMBROIDERY

With the edges of the fabric prepared and the
centre lines basted both ways, stretch the fabric in
a hoop, ready to work the cross stitching.

Referring to the chart given opposite and using
two strands of thread in the needle throughout,
finish the embroidery. For the stars, work eyelet
stitch (see diagram opposite). When working on an
openweave fabric, it is important to embroider each
star separately, and not to strand the thread across
the back, otherwise it will be clearly visible from
the right side.

Steam press the completed embroidery on the
wrong side. Do not remove the basting stitches at
this stage.

ASSEMBLING THE STAND

First, check to see if the template or card supplied
by the manufacturer will give an exact fit. This is
important, since the embroidery is simply cut out
to size and the raw edges covered by the wooden
frame; as you will see, this has a very shallow
recess and does not allow for the embroidery to be
cut too small.

To help you to centre your embroidery in the
frame, place the circular card supplied on the
embroidery chart and mark the centre both ways,
using a soft pencil. Next, place the embroidery face
down on a clean surface and, using the card as
a template, lay it on top, matching the basting

stitches to the pencil lines. Draw around the edge
with a soft pencil. Before cutting out, add any extra
fabric that may be required. Remove the basting
stitches and complete the assembly, following the
manufacturer's instructions.

STAR EYELET

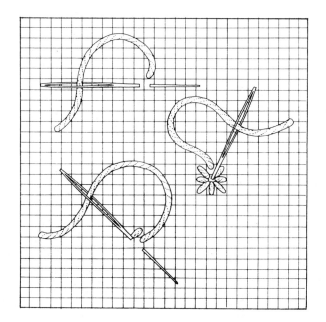

• Beginning at the top right corner, work eight
straight stitches over two threads (the length of the
particular cross stitch being worked), working from
the outer edge into the centre, as shown in the
diagram.

THE DONKEY ▲

- ◣ white
- I 3018 lemon (and stars)
- ◆ 783 deep gold (bks 781)
- ✹ 731 olive green
- △ 781 brown (bks on pannier)
- ○ 3072 light grey
- ⊡ 646 grey (bks 317)
- ● 317 dark grey (and hair of mane)
- ╱ 453 pale drab grey (bks on donkey's face)

$\mathscr{B}$ELLPULL

Worked on white linen and
supported with wooden rods, this
miniature bellpull can be hung
as a picture. If you have a real
bell to pull, however, it would be
fun to elongate the design,
adding more leaves and tendrills
as required.

JACK AND THE BEANSTALK

Eager to avenge his father's death, Jack
awoke very early one morning and, saying
goodbye to his dog, climbed the enormous
beanstalk in search of the wicked giant.

JACK AND THE BEANSTALK ▶

↑   831 deep yellow

⬤   739 flesh (bks 3708)

↓   3708 pale pink

| 3731 pink

●   3705 bright pink

△   3772 dusky pink (bks on leaves)

⊡   315 deep dusky pink (bks 367)

✱   498 red

S   518 blue (bks 367)

✕   472 pale green (bks on trousers 611)

|| 772 peppermint green

÷   471 green

=   581 olive green

◇   3364 moss green

◣   367 dark green (bks on bird's body
     and legs, tendrils around tree)

◆   611 brown (bks Jack's eye)

◸   452 dove grey (bks 647; bks on
     diamond-shaped windows 3041*)

○   647 grey

*Note: one additional backstitch colour**

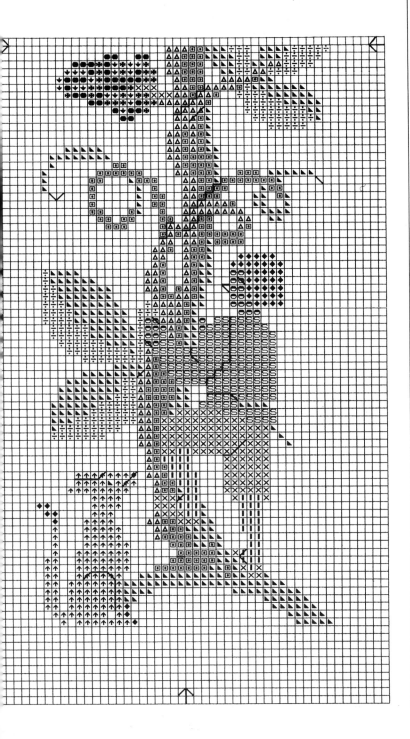

BELLPULL

YOU WILL NEED

For a bellpull measuring approximately
12cm × 43cm (4¾in × 17in):

*18cm × 56cm (7¼in × 22in) of natural-coloured
linen, 20 threads to 2.5cm (1in)
DMC stranded embroidery cotton in the colours
given in the panel
No 20 tapestry needle
60cm (24in) of white satin ribbon,
6mm (¼in) wide
Wooden rods, 13cm (5in) wide, for the bellpull
(for suppliers, see page 128)*

•

THE EMBROIDERY

Overcast the edges of the linen to prevent fraying, and with the centre marked both ways with basting stitches, stretch the fabric in a frame (see page 121). If you use a hoop, cover completed motifs with tissue paper to prevent the hoop from marking them.

Following the chart and colour key, complete the embroidery, using three strands of thread in the needle throughout and making each stitch over two threads. Steam press on the wrong side if needed.

MAKING UP THE BELLPULL

Trim the two long edges so that the total width across is 17cm (6¾in). Make 12mm (½in) double turnings on these edges, basting both the top and bottom edges of the turning to prevent the linen from slipping – a characteristic of some linens! Hem in place, using matching sewing thread.

On the two short edges, make a 2.5cm (1in) turning. Make a second turning, this time 4cm (1½in) deep, at each edge, taking the fabric over a rod at the top and bottom. Baste and hem in place.

Using double knots, on the inner side of the knobs, attach the ribbon to the top rod, leaving 8cm (3in) long ribbon tails to hang free, as shown in the photograph.

DRESSING-TABLE TRAY

This pretty glass-topped tray with its delightful cross-stitch design, would make a perfect accessory for a young girl's room.

LITTLE RED RIDING HOOD

Taking a basket of food and some flowers, Little Red Riding Hood set off to visit her sick grandmother, who lived in the next village. Just as she was taking a short cut through the wood, she heard the gruff voice of the wolf saying, 'Where are you going Little Red Riding Hood?'

RED RIDING HOOD ▲

Ͱ white (bks 597)	✕ 729 gold	÷ 948 flesh	✲ 347 red (bks 869)	◣ 597 turquoise
◇ 726 yellow	✦ 977 orange	▣ 223 pink	‖ 747 pale blue	(and bks smok
◺ 833 light gold	= 782 deep orange	❙ 3328 light red	(bks 597)	bks 869)

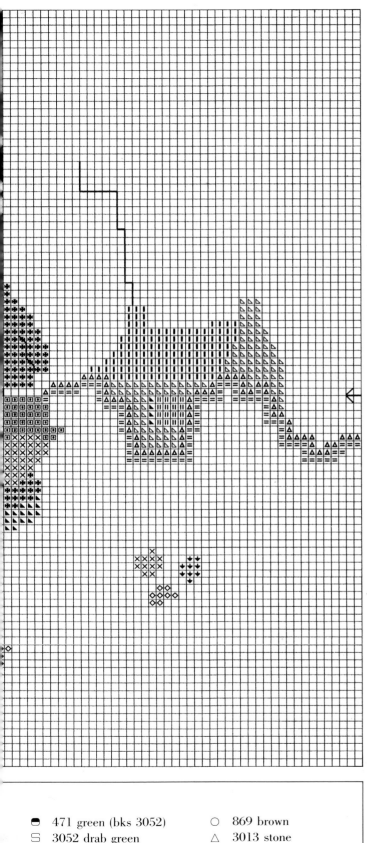

DRESSING-TABLE TRAY

YOU WILL NEED

For a rectangular tray measuring 23cm × 30cm
(9in × 12in) with a 18cm × 25cm (7¼in × 10in)
oval cut out:

*38cm × 30cm (15in × 12in) of grey evenweave
(Aida 718) fabric, 14 threads to 2.5cm (1in)
DMC stranded embroidery cotton in the colours
given in the panel
No24 tapestry needle
Wooden tray (for suppliers, see page 128)*

•

THE EMBROIDERY

Mark the fabric both ways with basting stitches and
prepare the edges before stretching it in a frame.
Following the chart, complete the cross stitching,
using two strands of thread in the needle throughout. Finish by adding the backstitch details on top.

Remove the embroidery from the frame and, if
needed, steam press on the wrong side.

ASSEMBLING THE TRAY

Where the recess is deep enough, as is the case
with this tray, an embroidery can be stretched over
the supplied card, which you may find preferable
to cutting the fabric close to the embroidery.

To centre the card over the embroidery, first mark
the card both ways, using a soft pencil. Place the
embroidery face down with the card on top, basting
and pencil lines matching.

Begin by folding over the fabric at each corner
and securing it with masking tape. Working on one
side and then on the opposite side, fold over the
edges of the fabric on all sides and secure with
pieces of masking tape, leaving the corners at this
stage (see page 123). Check to see that the embroidery is centred; if not, simply release the masking
tape and readjust the position. Neaten the corners
by folding them over to form a mitre and secure
with masking tape.

Insert the mounted embroidery into the tray,
following the manufacturer's instructions.

⊟	471 green (bks 3052)	○	869 brown
S	3052 drab green	△	3013 stone
◆	371 light brown (bks 413)	●	413 dark grey

Make this charming set of tiny cushions to scatter on a young teenager's bed, or mix them with other cushions to fill an armchair or sofa.

THE PIED PIPER

RUMPLESTILTSKIN

THE GOOSEGIRL

SCATTER CUSHIONS

YOU WILL NEED

For three cushion covers, each measuring
24cm (9½in) square:

*58cm × 29cm (23in × 11½in) each of cream,
pink and grey evenweave Aida fabric,
14 threads to 2.5cm (1in)
100cm (40in) each of gold (metallic), grey and red
fabric-covered piping
DMC stranded embroidery cotton in the colours
given in the panels on pages 37, 40 and 41
No24 tapestry needle
Matching sewing threads
Three 25cm (10in) square cushion pads
Tracing paper*

•

THE EMBROIDERY

All three cushions are made in the same way. To
make one cushion, cut the evenweave fabric in half
to give two pieces, each measuring 29cm (11½in)
square. Following the instructions given on page
121, prepare and stretch one of the pieces of fabric
in an embroidery frame.

Referring to the appropriate chart, and colour
key, complete the cross stitching, using two strands
of thread in the needle throughout, and working the
backstitch details on top. Finish by backstitching
the outline around the design, working each quarter
section symmetrically, and again, using two strands
of the thread in the needle.

Remove the embroidery from the frame and
steam press on the wrong side.

MAKING UP THE CUSHION COVER

Trim the edges of the embroidery and the backing
section of evenweave so that they each measure
26.5cm (10½in) square. Following the outline of
the cushion corner given with the chart for the Pied
Piper, make a template from tracing paper, rever-
sing each corner on the centre lines to complete the
cushion shape. Using the template, mark and then
cut around the curved corners on both sections of

evenweave fabric. A 12mm (½in) seam allowance
is included.

Metallic gold piping has been used for the
Rumplestiltskin design, red for the Pied Piper and
grey for The Goosegirl. Lay the piping on the right
side of the embroidery, placing the raw edge just
inside the seam allowance. Baste, and then use the
piping foot to machine stitch it in place (see page
123). Overlap the two ends, neatly angling the raw
edges into the seam allowance. If the piping can be
spliced (unlike purchased metallic varieties), this
would give an invisible join, see page 123.

With right sides of the cushion front and back
together, baste and machine stitch around the
edges, leaving a 16cm (6¼in) opening in the
middle of one side, again using the piping foot, and
stitching as close as possible to the piping.

Remove the basting threads, snip into the
corners and turn the cover to the right side. Before
inserting the cushion pad, give the corners a
slightly rounded shape by tucking in the point of
each corner by about 12mm (½in). Finger-press
the resultant rounded shaping for about 4cm (1½in)
on each side of the point, gently easing the curve
into the side seams at each corner. Loosely overcast
the seam to hold the shape. Insert the cushion pad,
turn in the opening and slipstitch to close, using
matching sewing thread.

PIED PIPER ▶

↑ 725 yellow
◣ 741 amber
Ⅰ 370 ochre (bks 317)
S 3779 flesh (bks 927)
✱ 606 red (bks 317)
⊡ 309 magenta (bks 317)
◿ 703 green
○ 943 veridian green (bks 317)
● 3052 drab green
◆ 927 light grey (bks 317)
↓ 317 grey (rat's feet; bks 927)
△ 413 dark grey (all whiskers and
    piper's moustache)

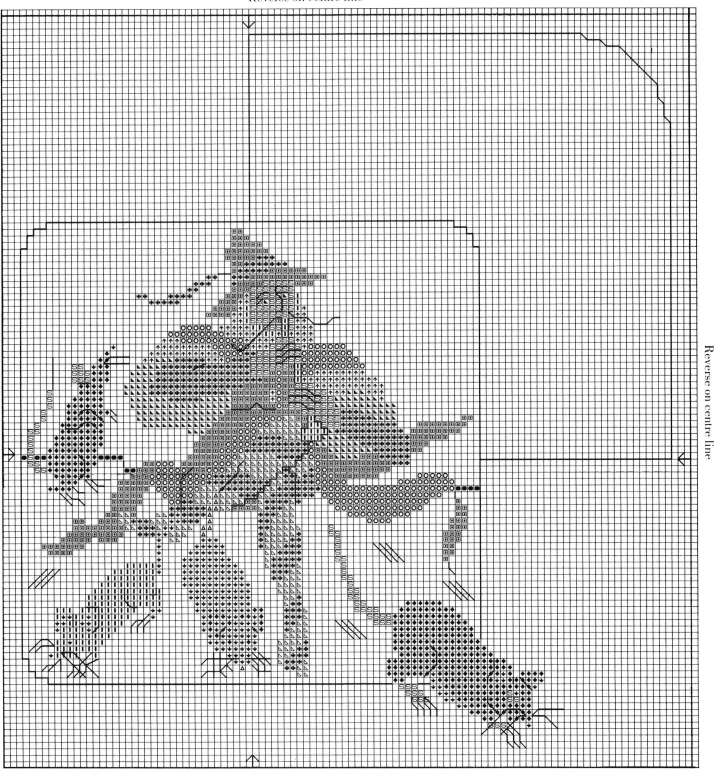

THE PIED PIPER

The Pied Piper put his brass flute to his lips and began to play a
sad, haunting melody. Suddenly, the streets of Hamelin seethed
with rats; the Pied Piper walked towards the river and sat down,
whereupon the rats threw themselves into the icy water and
disappeared forever.

THE GOOSEGIRL

The princess, tricked by her servant into minding geese, speaks to the head of her horse Falada. Every morning, as she sets out to tend her flock of geese, she stops at the gateway and says, 'Alas, dear Falada, there you hang.' And Falada answers, 'Alas, Queen's daughter, there you go, if your mother knew your fate, her heart would break with grief so great.' Then she goes on her way till she comes to the common, where she sits down and begins to comb out her hair.

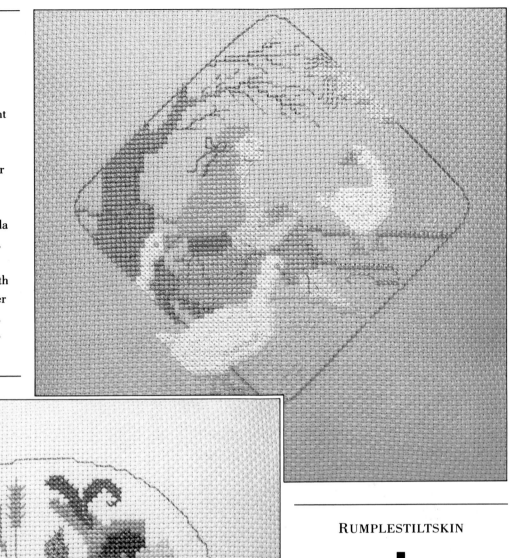

RUMPLESTILTSKIN

Appearing suddenly, as if from nowhere, the rather eccentric and diminutive little man asked the miller's daughter, 'What will you give me if I spin the straw into gold?' 'The ring from my finger', she replied. Rumplestiltskin hopped onto the stool and began to spin. In just a few minutes he had changed the pile of straw into a hundred bobbins of pure gold thread.

RUMPLESTILTSKIN ▲

S 834 corn (and bks stems)

✦ 725 yellow (bks 3045)

○ gold thread (and thread being spun; bks 3045)

◆ 3779 flesh (bks 3011)

● 3712 red (bks 3766)

◣ 3753 pale turquoise (bks 3766)

▣ 3766 turquoise (bks 3347)

❙ 3347 green

△ 3045 light brown (bks 3011)

✳ 3011 brown (bks 3045)

THE GOOSEGIRL ▼

- = white (bks 3072)
- ◆ 725 yellow (bks 3013)
- ↑ 834 gold (bks 725)
- | 948 flesh (bks 3706; bks eye 927)
- ● 3354 dusky pink (bks outline around design)
- ◺ 3706 deep pink (bks hair ribbon)

- ○ 927 drab turquoise (bks 3354)
- ⩘ 772 pale green (bks grass)
- ↓ 3013 olive green
- ⊡ 3052 drab green (bks tree branches)
- △ 3072 grey (bks 927 on sleeve; bks 926 on horse)
- ✱ 926 dark grey

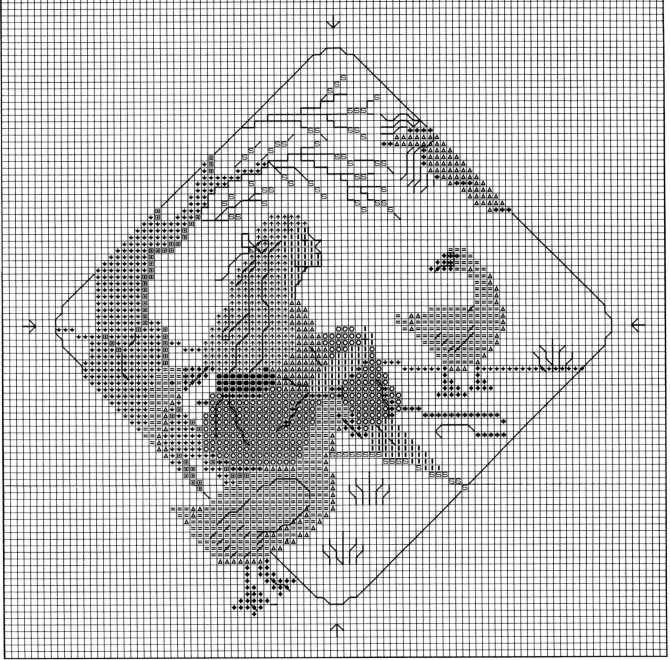

VICTORIAN MOUNTS

Capturing the Victorian style
of decorated picture mounts,
these can be used to give a
traditional effect to whatever
you wish to frame.

THE GOLDEN BIRD

THE ELVES AND THE SHOEMAKER

SNOW WHITE AND ROSE RED

VICTORIAN MOUNTS

YOU WILL NEED

For one picture mount with an overall measurement of 24cm × 19cm (9½in × 7½in); this includes 6mm (¼in) all around, for fitting into the recess of a picture frame:

30cm × 25cm (12in × 10in) of cream linen, 26 threads to 2.5cm (1in)
DMC stranded embroidery cotton in the colours given in the panels on pages 45, 48 and 49
24cm × 19cm (9½in × 7½in) of lightweight synthetic batting
30cm × 25cm (12in × 10in) of lightweight iron-on interfacing
24cm × 19cm (9½ × 7½in) of thin mounting card
Craft knife or sharp general purpose scissors
No26 tapestry needle and No9 crewel needle
Matching sewing threads
Tracing paper
Spray glue
All-purpose clear glue
Picture frame of your choice with a window area measuring 23cm × 18cm (9in × 7in)

•

THE EMBROIDERY

All three mounts are made in the same way. The individual colour keys, given with the charts, show clearly where metallic threads, beads and pearls are used, and list the quantities. Following the instructions given on page 121, stretch the prepared fabric in a rectangular frame.

Using two strands of embroidery thread in the needle, and referring to the appropriate chart, complete the cross stitching. Remove the work from the frame and press the interfacing to the wrong side of the fabric. Using the crewel needle and matching thread, add the beads and pearls to the Elves and the Shoemaker and to Snow White the Rose Red respectively (see page 125).

If necessary, steam press the finished embroidery on the right side, protecting it with a dry cloth, and taking care not to press too heavily over the beads and pearls.

COMPLETING THE MOUNT

To give a slightly padded look to the finished mount, a thin layer of batting is placed between the embroidery and the mounting card.

Using a soft pencil (2B), begin by tracing both the inner and outer lines of the frame given with the chart. Turn over the tracing; centre it on the card, and trace through. Carefully cut out the window area, using a craft knife.

Cut the batting to the same shape as the mount, using the latter as a template, and then attach it to the mount with spray glue.

Mount the fabric, following the instructions for the Dressing-Table Tray (see page 33). With the wrong side facing, cut horizontally and vertically, and then cut diagonally across the centre both ways, cutting through both layers and snipping right up to the corners and to within 6mm (¼in) of the window edge. You will find that one or two tiny spots of clear glue, placed at the corners of the card, will help to secure the cut threads of the fabric. Trim across the flaps to straighten them, leaving allowances 12mm (½in) deep. Working on opposite sides, fold the allowances to the back of the card and secure them firmly with masking tape.

Centre your chosen photograph or painting behind the mount, securing it with masking tape before inserting the mount into the picture frame.

THE GOLDEN BIRD ▶

△ gold thread (bks 3052)
⊡ 3013 green (bks around tree and twigs)
✱ 3053 drab green
● 3052 dark drab green

The king had a beautiful pleasure garden around his palace, in which grew a very special tree that bore golden apples. As the apples ripened, they were counted, but every morning one was missing. The king sent his first and second sons in turn to guard the tree, but they fell asleep, and in the morning more apples were missing. It was now the turn of the youngest son. As the clock struck midnight, there was a rustling in the air, and by the light of the moon, the young prince saw a bird whose shining feathers were of pure gold. Just as the bird was plucking an apple, the prince shot an arrow at it. The bird escaped unhurt, but a golden feather dropped to the ground.

THE ELVES AND THE SHOEMAKER

The ageing shoemaker spent all day cutting out a pair of shoes from his last pieces of leather. He went to bed, leaving the cut-out shapes on his workbench. In the morning, to his surprise, he saw a finished pair of shoes in their place, perfect to the last shining buckle. Someone had made the shoes for him overnight!

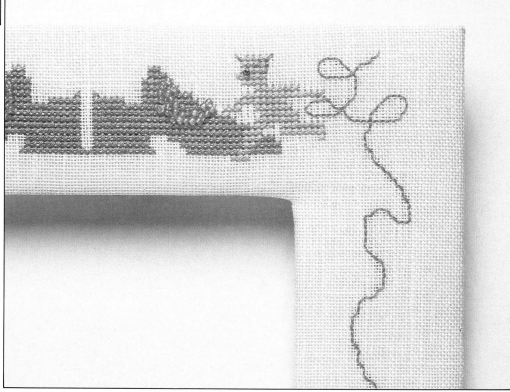

SNOW WHITE AND
ROSE RED

Every morning in summer, and before her
mother awoke, Rose Red placed a bunch of
flowers beside her bed, taking roses from each
tree that grew in their cottage garden.

THE ELVES AND THE SHOEMAKER ▲

- ⊡   788 pale pink (bks 3733)
- △   788 with matching glass beads
- ●   3733 pink (bks sewing thread; bks 452)
- ✢   452 drab mauve (bks sewing needles and cotton reels)

SNOW WHITE AND ROSE RED ▶

- ↑   white (bks 452)
- ╱   white seed pearls
- ⊐   726 yellow
- Ⅰ   725 deep yellow
- ◣   761 pink (bks thorns and stems)
- ●   352 deep pink (bks around pink flowers)
- △   3013 sage green
- ○   733 green
- ✳   924 dark green
- ◆   3072 pale grey
- ↓   452 grey (bks thorns and stems)
- ⊡   451 dark grey

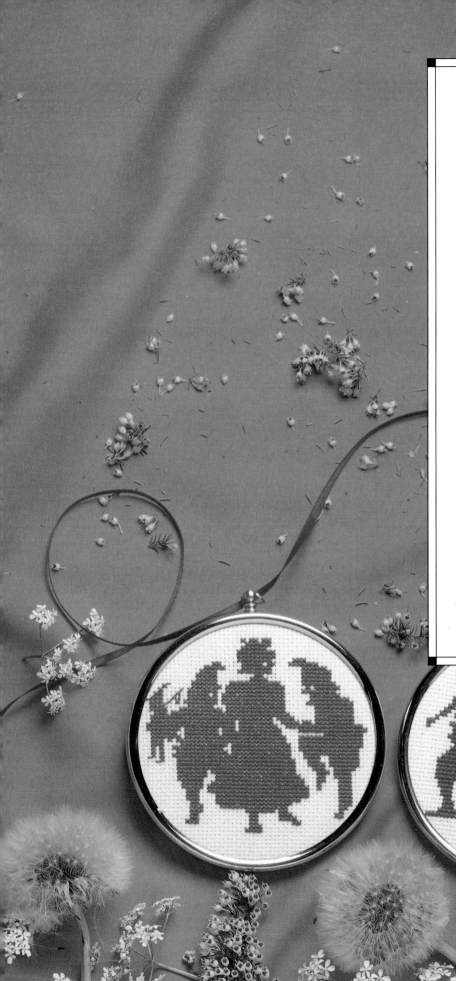

WALL MIRROR AND MINIATURE PICTURES

'Mirror, mirror on the wall!' – this delightful wall mirror could be the starting point for a collection of silhouettes.

❖

SNOW WHITE AND THE SEVEN DWARFS

'Tell me, glass, tell me true!
Of all the ladies in the land,
Who is the fairest? tell me who?
And the glass answered,
'Thou, queen, art the fairest in all this land;
But over the hills, in the greenwood shade,
Where seven dwarfs their home have made,
There Snow White is hiding her head, and she
Is lovelier far, O queen! than thee'.

WALL MIRROR AND MINIATURE PICTURES

YOU WILL NEED

For a wooden wall mirror with an overall measurement of 39.5cm × 13cm (15½ × 5in) and a cross stitch area of 13cm × 9cm (5in × 3½in), and two brass-framed miniatures each measuring 10cm (4in) in diameter:

60cm × 20cm (24in × 8in) of pale blue evenweave Aida fabric, 16 threads to 2.5cm (1in)
DMC stranded embroidery cotton: 3 skeins of 3350
No26 tapestry needle
Wall mirror and two miniature picture frames
(for suppliers, see page 128)

●

THE EMBROIDERY

You can either stitch all three designs with the single piece of fabric stretched in a rectangular frame, or use a hoop for the individual designs. Whichever you decide, first divide the fabric into three equal sections, each measuring 20cm (8in) square, either cutting the fabric or marking the divisions with basting stitches. Baste the centre both ways on each section, ready for the embroidery. Referring to the charts and, using two strands of the thread in the needle, complete the cross stitching.

Remove from the frame and, if needed, steam press the finished embroidery on the wrong side. Cut out each section along the dividing lines.

ASSEMBLING THE MIRROR AND PICTURES

For the mirror, mount the embroidery following the instructions given for the Dressing-Table Tray on page 33. Complete the assembly, following the manufacturer's instructions.
For the miniature pictures, first place the circular card template over the chart and mark the centre both ways, using a soft pencil. Lay the embroidery face down with the card on top, matching basting stitches and lines, and draw around the card with pencil. Working freehand, draw a second line about 4cm (1½in) outside, and cut out along this outer line.

With double sewing thread in the needle, make a line of running stitches about 2cm (¾in) in from the raw edge, close to the marked line. Place the card on the wrong side and pull up the thread, spacing the gathers evenly, and making sure the fabric grain is straight. Secure the thread firmly. Add pieces of masking tape over the edges of the fabric for extra strength.

Finish the assembly, following the manufacturer's instructions.

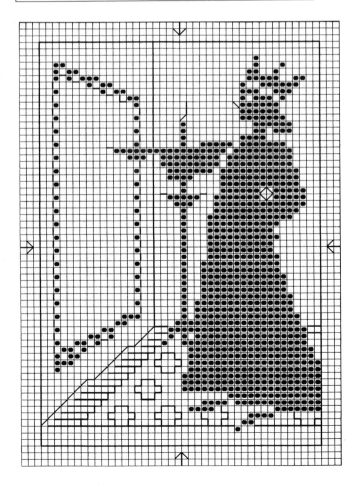

SNOW WHITE AND THE SEVEN DWARFS ▼ MIRROR

● 3350 (and bks details)

MINIATURE PICTURE ▼

● 3350 (and bks details)

MINIATURE PICTURE ▲

● 3350 (and bks details)

PAPER-WEIGHTS

Made from small remnants of linen, these charming little paperweights are perfect starting points for beginners.

TOWN MOUSE AND COUNTRY MOUSE

Every day country mouse busied herself in the fields collecting grains of corn and wild berries. But one day she visited her cousin in town . . . 'Now sit yourself down' said the town mouse 'and I'll bring you the most delicious feast you've ever had – apple pie, chocolate cake, biscuits and china tea,' saying nothing of the large tabby cat who also lived in the house.

PAPERWEIGHTS

YOU WILL NEED

For two paperweights, one an oval measuring 10cm × 8cm (4in × 3in), and the other circular, measuring 9cm (3½in) in diameter:

25cm × 15cm (10in × 6in) of natural linen, 21 threads to 2.5cm (1in)
DMC stranded embroidery cotton in the colours given in the panels on pages 56 and 57
No26 tapestry needle
Glass-topped paperweights
(for suppliers, see page 128)

If you are embroidering both designs on one piece of fabric, begin by preparing the edges and stretching it in a rectangular frame. Otherwise, divide the fabric in half, overcast the edges, and set each piece in a hoop.

Baste the centre both ways for each design. Following the charts and colour keys given opposite, complete the embroidery, using two strands of thread in the needle throughout. Work the cross stitching first and then finish with the backstitch details. Remember when embroidering on very openweave fabric not to strand across the back, otherwise the threads will be visible on the right side. Remove the finished embroidery from the frame and steam press on the wrong side.

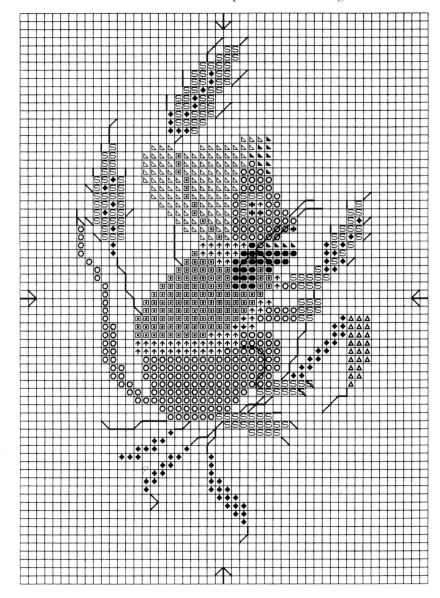

COUNTRY MOUSE ▶

↑   white
S   3046 straw (bks feet)
◣   224 pink
●   3731 deep pink
◺   828 pale turquoise
⊡   518 deep turquoise
△   3053 sap green (bks leaves)
○   3045 brown (bks 413)
◆   772 stone (bks corn stems and whiskers)
↓   762 grey
✳   413 dark grey (bks whiskers)

MOUNTING FABRIC OVER A PAPER TEMPLATE

The manufacturer suggests mounting the cut-out embroidery and securing it underneath with the felt backing supplied. This is a suitable method for fine fabrics, but with a medium-weight linen, the raw edges can clearly be seen, giving a slightly frayed look. To overcome this, simply mount the fabric over the paper template supplied.

Place the paper template over the chart and mark the centre both ways, using a soft pencil. Lay the embroidery face down with the template on top, matching basting stitches and centre lines. Draw around the edge with the pencil. Working freehand, draw a second line about 2.5cm (1in) outside, and cut out along this line.

Using sewing thread in the needle, make a line of running stitches about 12mm (½in) in from the raw edge. Place the paper template on the wrong side and pull up the thread, spacing the gathers evenly, and making sure the grain of the fabric is straight and the design is centred.

ASSEMBLING THE PAPERWEIGHTS

Following the instructions given for the Miniature Pictures on page 52, mount the embroidery, and then finish the assembly, according to manufacturer's instructions.

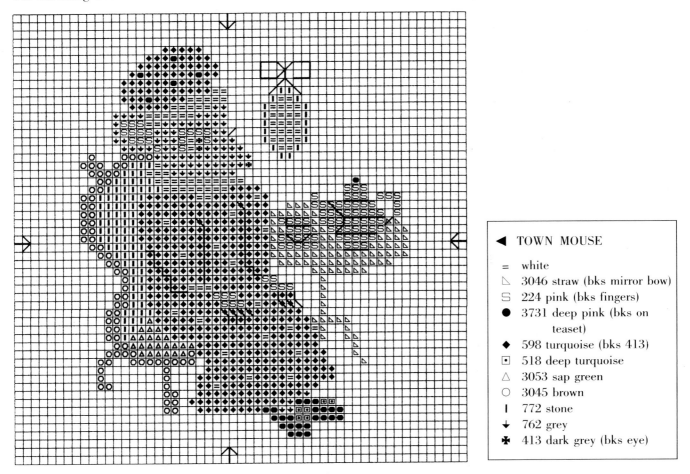

◀ TOWN MOUSE

= white
◺ 3046 straw (bks mirror bow)
S 224 pink (bks fingers)
● 3731 deep pink (bks on teaset)
◆ 598 turquoise (bks 413)
⊡ 518 deep turquoise
△ 3053 sap green
○ 3045 brown
I 772 stone
↓ 762 grey
✳ 413 dark grey (bks eye)

CANDLE SCREEN AND BOOKMARK

Embroider this delicate little candle screen, with its eastern design, and the accompanying bookmark to evoke days gone by – a timely reminder of the many leisurely hours that people used to spend reading by candlelight.

THE NIGHTINGALE

Longing to return to her brothers and sisters, the nightingale escaped from her cage by pretending to be dead. When her rich, Persian owner laid her on the grass she soared quickly into the sky and flew back to her home in the forest.

THE MERMAID WHO COULDN'T SWIM

Melinda, the little mermaid hung on tightly as the dolphin raced effortlessly over the waves. 'I will carry you far across the sea. I will take you anywhere you wish.'

CANDLE SCREEN

YOU WILL NEED

For a candle screen approximately 46cm (18in) high with an adjustable screen and design area 12.5 cm × 9cm (4¾ × 3½in):

20cm × 15cm (8in × 6in) of blue evenweave Aida fabric, 14 threads to 2.5cm (1in)
DMC stranded embroidery cotton in the colours given in the appropriate panel
No24 tapestry needle
Wooden candle screen
(for suppliers, see page 128)

•

THE EMBROIDERY

Mark the centre of the fabric both ways with basting stitches, and prepare the edges, then stretch it in a frame (see page 121).

Following the chart, and using two strands of thread in the needle throughout, complete the cross stitching, then work the backstitch details on top.

When embroidering this type of scenic design, it is always a good idea to stitch the foreground, such as the tree on the left, before the background. And also, where very light and dark colours are involved in a design, it is always better to embroider the lighter colours last of all, to minimize handling, and the risk of dirtying the thread. Obviously, while your embroidery is not being worked, it is advisable to keep it covered up.

Remove the finished embroidery from the frame and press it on the wrong side.

ASSEMBLING THE CANDLE SCREEN

Mount the embroidery on the supplied card, following the instructions given for the Dressing-Table Tray on page 33. Follow the manufacturer's instructions to finish the assembly.

BOOKMARK

YOU WILL NEED

For a bookmark measuring about 25cm × 9cm (10in × 3½in):

One ready-made lace-edged cream bookmark with a Hardanger centre, 16 threads to 2.5cm (1in) (for suppliers, see page 128)
DMC stranded embroidery cotton in the colours given in the appropriate panel
No26 tapestry needle

•

THE EMBROIDERY

Using oddments from your scrap bag, baste small pieces of fabric to the long edges of the bookmark. Either stretch it in a hoop, see page 120, or simply push drawing-pins through the fabric pieces to attach the work to a canvas stretcher.

There are some professional embroiderers who prefer to work cross stitch in the hand, and provided you keep an eye on your stitching tension, this small bookmark may be the exception to the general rule that it is advisable to hold the work in a frame of some kind.

With centre lines basted, and following the chart given opposite, complete the embroidery, using two strands of thread in the needle throughout.

Remove the basting threads and steam press on the wrong side.

It would be quite easy to make your own bookmarks for cross stitching, from oddments of evenweave left over from other projects.

You could machine zigzag stitch broderie anglaise or lace trim around the edges, and on the lower edge, add a similar ribbon marker in colours of your choice. These would not only be your own creation, but would be an inexpensive and economical way of using up leftovers — and perhaps, a quick and easy project to make for the next bazaar you are asked to support!

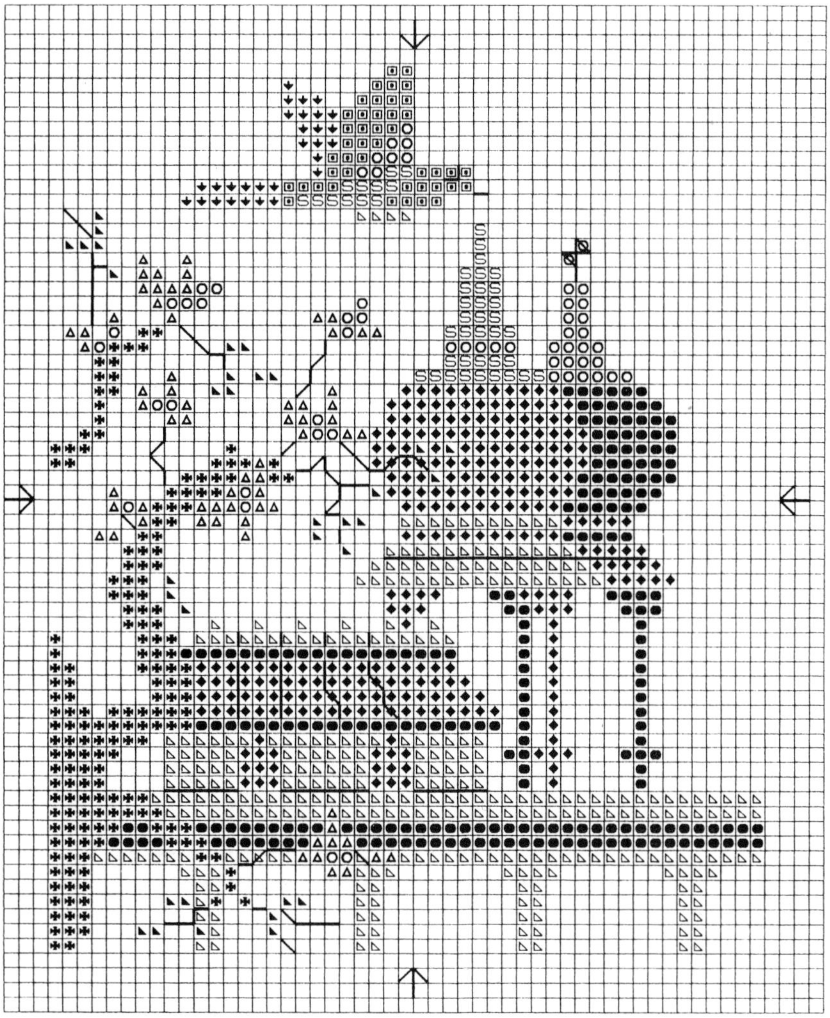

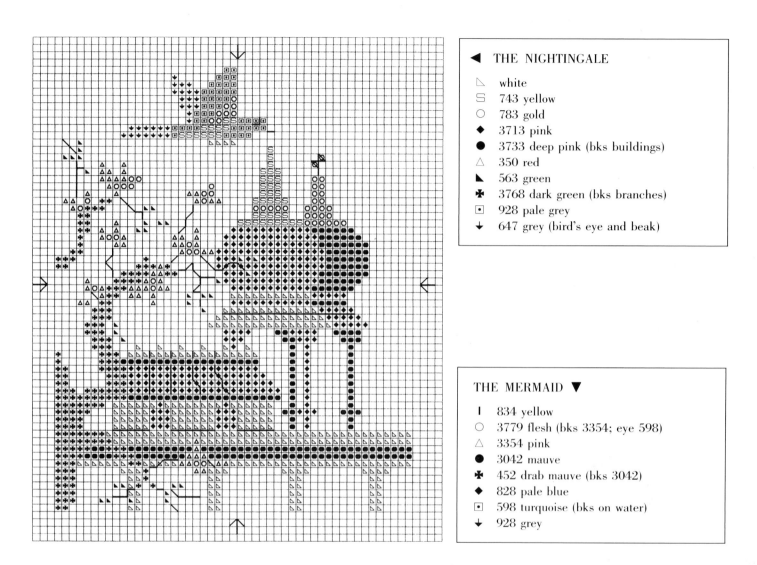

◀ THE NIGHTINGALE

◺	white
S	743 yellow
○	783 gold
◆	3713 pink
●	3733 deep pink (bks buildings)
△	350 red
◣	563 green
✙	3768 dark green (bks branches)
⊡	928 pale grey
↓	647 grey (bird's eye and beak)

THE MERMAID ▼

I	834 yellow
○	3779 flesh (bks 3354; eye 598)
△	3354 pink
●	3042 mauve
✙	452 drab mauve (bks 3042)
◆	828 pale blue
⊡	598 turquoise (bks on water)
↓	928 grey

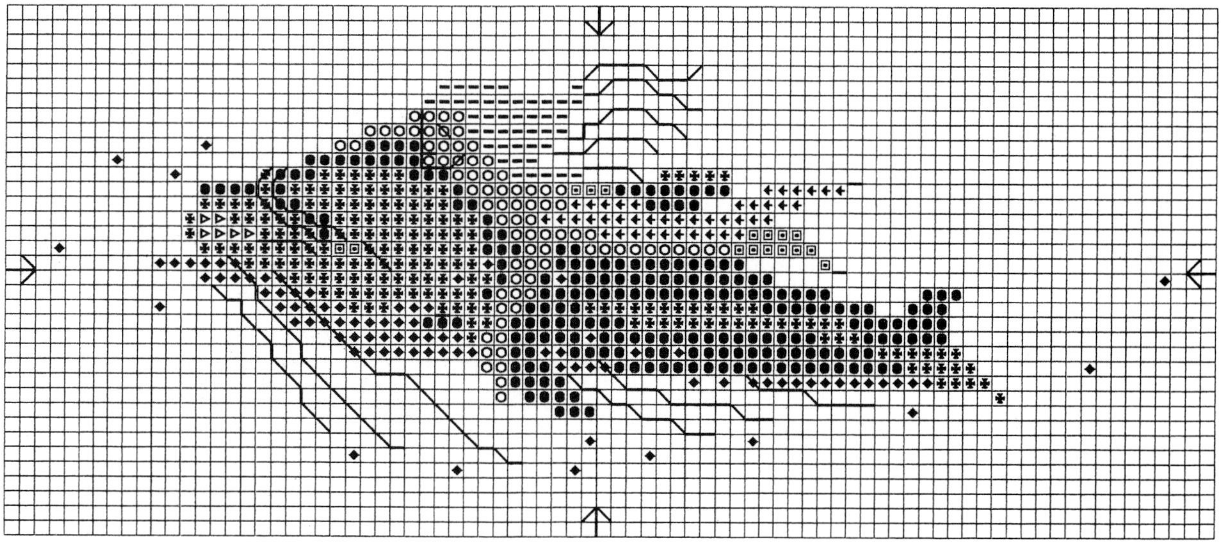

TRADITIONAL SAMPLER

The enduring appeal of the
sampler – worked here in the
traditional style, with borders
and motifs in a single colour –
will ensure that this delightful
picture of the twelve dancing
princesses becomes a favourite
gift for family and friends.

THE TWELVE DANCING PRINCESSES

The King's twelve daughters secretly danced
all night, until their shoes were worn through.
In order to find out where they danced and
with whom, the King allowed a soldier to spy
on them. The soldier discovers that they are
being taken by princes across a lake to
an underground castle, and his reward is to
marry the eldest princess, with whom he lives
happily ever after.

DANCING PRINCESSES ▲

3047 cream (bks on castle walls)   ● 349 red (and bks details)

TRADITIONAL SAMPLER

YOU WILL NEED

For a sampler measuring 24cm × 29cm
(9½in × 11½in):

*35cm × 40cm (14in × 16in) of pale khaki
evenweave Aida fabric, or linen,
16 threads to 2.5cm (1in)
DMC stranded embroidery cotton in the colour given
in the panel, plus 3 skeins of red 349, used for
the main colour
No24 tapestry needle
24cm × 29cm (9½in × 11½in) of lightweight
synthetic batting
24cm × 29cm (9½in × 11½in) of
medium-weight mounting board
Spray glue
Picture frame of your choice*

•

THE EMBROIDERY

With the prepared fabric stretched in a frame, see
page 121, and the centre lines basted both ways,
begin the embroidery. Using two strands of thread
in the needle, and carefully following the chart,
complete the cross stitching.

Remove the finished embroidery from the
frame; take out the basting stitches, and steam
press the work on the wrong side.

FRAMING THE SAMPLER

For a slightly padded effect, a thin layer of batting
is placed between the embroidery and the mounting board. Cut the batting to the same size as the
mounting board and attach it to the board with
spray glue or fabric adhesive. Mount the embroidery, following the instructions given for the
Dressing-Table Tray on page 33.

Insert the glass and the mounted embroidery
into your picture frame; add the backing board
provided, and tack in place. Cover the tacks with
broad sticky tape to neaten, and your sampler is
ready to hang up.

Of princes and princesses

Traditional tales of love and adventure have been captured in this delightful set of cushions.

SLEEPING BEAUTY

THE SWINEHERD

BEAUTY AND THE BEAST

OF PRINCES
AND PRINCESSES

YOU WILL NEED

For three cushion covers, each measuring
27.5cm (11in) square:

*35cm (14in) square each of apple green,
pink and cream evenweave Aida fabric,
14 threads to 2.5cm (1in)
30cm (12in) square each of matching or contrast
backing fabric
DMC stranded emboidery cotton in the colours
given in the panels on pages 69, 72 and 73
3 × 30cm (12in) square cushion pads
28 white seed pearls for the Swineherd design
No24 tapestry needle and No9 crewel needle
Matching sewing threads*

•

THE EMBROIDERY

All three cushions are made in the following way.
For one cushion, stretch the prepared fabric in a
frame, see page 121, and baste the centre lines in
both directions.

Using two strands of thread in the needle, and
following the appropriate chart, complete the cross
stitching. Also work the backstitching with two
strands of thread in the needle, with the exception
of the following details which are worked with a
single strand: Beauty and the Beast – the beast's
teeth and tusks; Sleeping Beauty – Beauty's face
and hands and her dress, and the prince's face. The
pearls around the Swineherd design are sewn on
with matching sewing thread and a fine crewel
needle (see page 125).

Complete the embroidery by backstitching the
outline around the design, using two strands of
thread in the needle. Remove the finished embroidery from the frame and steam press on the wrong
side. Do not over press the pearls.

MAKING UP THE CUSHION

Using the basting threads as a guide, trim the edges
of the embroidery symmetrically to measure 30cm

(12in) square. Place the backing fabric and the
embroidery right sides together, baste and machine
stitch around the edges, taking a 12mm (½in)
seam, and leaving a 20cm (8in) opening in the
middle of one side.

Trim across the corners and turn the cover
through to the right side. Insert the cushion pad
and, using matching sewing thread, slipstitch the
opening to close.

Attach a small tassel to each corner of the border.
To make a tassel, wind matching embroidery thread
(six strands) five or six times around a narrow piece
of card, about 2cm (¾in) wide. Thread a needle
with a short length of thread (two strands), slip the
threads off the card and wind the thread several
times around, close to the top, as in the diagram
shown below. Pass the needle through the loops at
the top and repeat a second time. Pull the thread
firmly and bring the needle up through the centre,
ready to sew the tassel in place.

Cut through the loops at the bottom of the tassel;
fan out the threads, and trim across. Neatly stitch
a tassel to each corner, as shown in the photograph.

MAKING A TASSEL

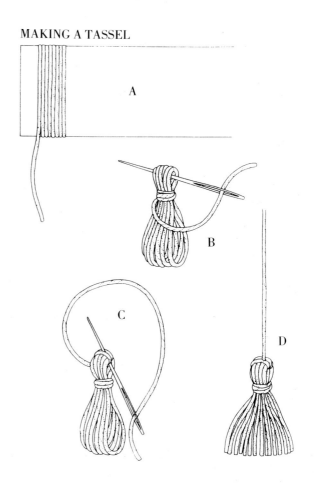

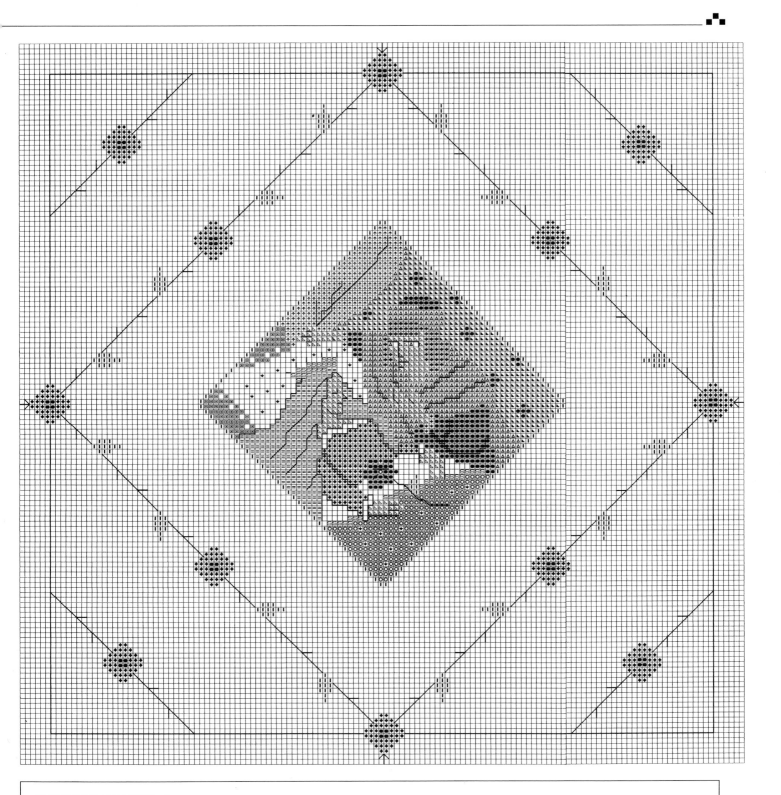

SLEEPING BEAUTY ▲

□ white

= 3078 pale yellow (bks 743)

○ 743 yellow

⊑ 733 gold (bks on Beauty's face and hands, and outer lines on hair)

↓ gold thread

◺ 754 flesh (bks 732 for prince)

● 351 red (bks around Beauty's dress and the mouths of both figures)

◆ 747 pale blue

△ 924 dark blue (bks 504)

↑ 504 pale green

▏ 581 green (ground pattern and thorns)

✳ 732 deep olive (bks on prince's face)

◣ 644 fawn

⊡ 613 light brown

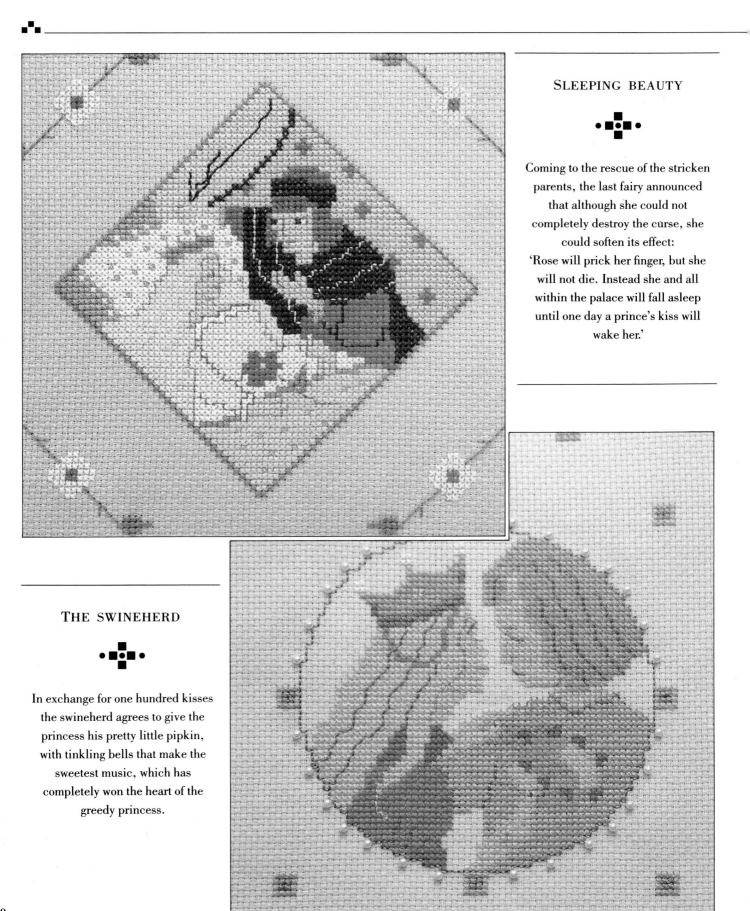

Coming to the rescue of the stricken
parents, the last fairy announced
that although she could not
completely destroy the curse, she
could soften its effect:
'Rose will prick her finger, but she
will not die. Instead she and all
within the palace will fall asleep
until one day a prince's kiss will
wake her.'

THE SWINEHERD

In exchange for one hundred kisses
the swineherd agrees to give the
princess his pretty little pipkin,
with tinkling bells that make the
sweetest music, which has
completely won the heart of the
greedy princess.

BEAUTY AND THE BEAST

Remembering her dream, Beauty flew to the
garden where she found poor Beast stretched
out, quite senseless, as though dead. 'Beast,
oh Beast,' she wept, lifting his huge head onto
her lap. 'You must not die, I love you.'

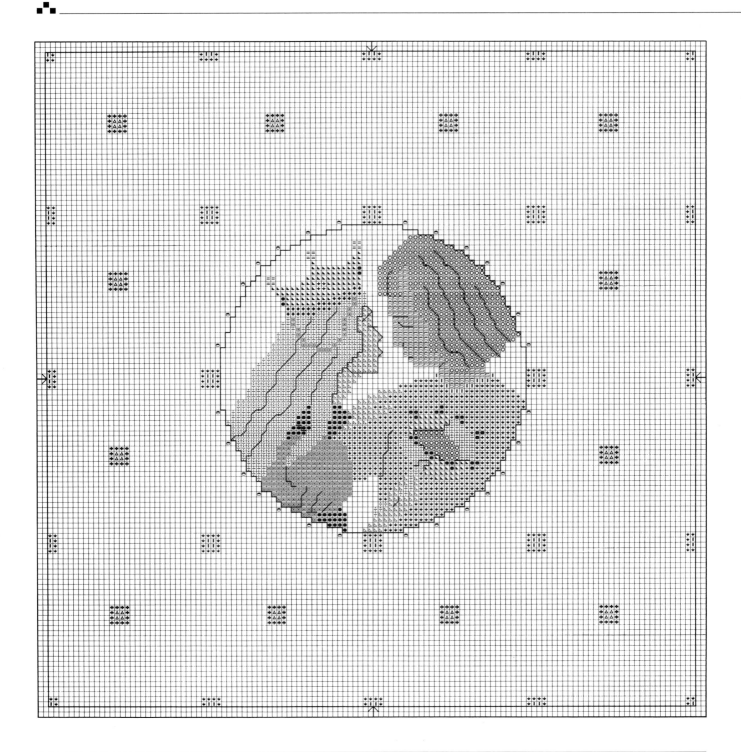

THE SWINEHERD ▲

= white

● white seed pearls

○ 834 pale gold (bks 680)

÷ 744 yellow (bks 680)

◆ 680 gold (princess'
eyebrows)

◣ 725 deep yellow (bks
hair line next to
princess' face)

�⊑ 3779 flesh (bks 680)

◺ 963 pale pink (bks 605;
bks princess' eye
959)

✳ 605 sugar pink

⊡ 3706 peach pink
(bks 603)

● 603 deep pink

△ 3609 dull pink

↓ 959 veridian green
(bks 3364)

Ɩ 3364 green (bks circle
outline and the
square outlining
the design)

□   white
÷   727 pale yellow (bks on
    shawl and dress cuff)
◣   3046 pale gold (bks
    on dress)

◤   783 yellow
↑   948 flesh (bks 224)
I   3713 pale pink
✳   224 dusky pink
△   352 pink

●   3075 red (bks on snout;
    bks 731)
◆   680 ginger (bks around
    feather)
=   747 pale blue

S   3053 sage green
⊡   731 dark olive
↓   3051 very dark olive
○   3045 light brown
    (bks 731)

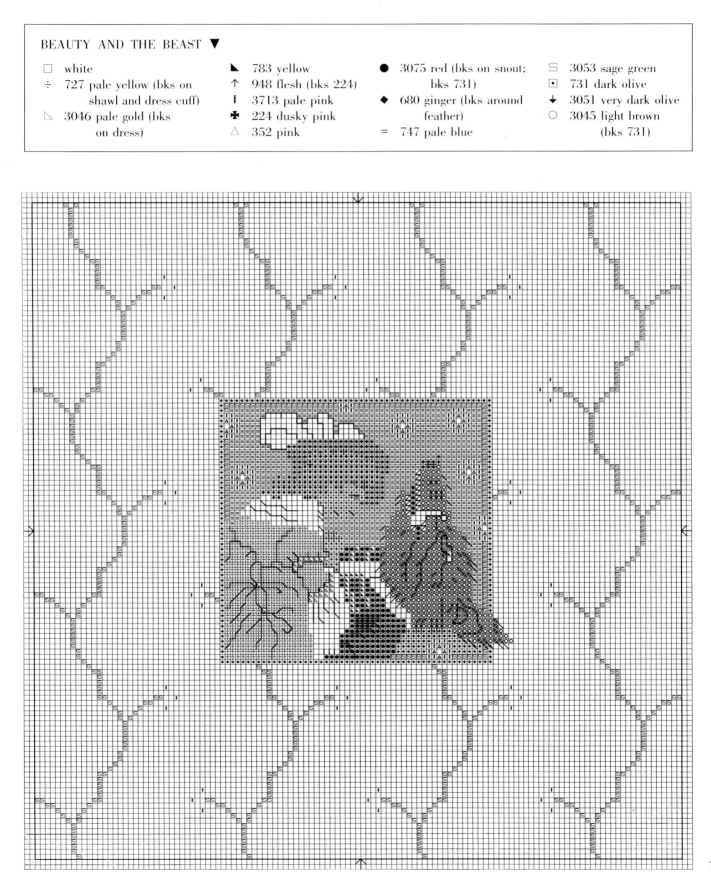

$\mathscr{P}$RESERVE-POT COVERS

Made from washable cotton,
these pretty, lace-edged covers
are quick and easy to embroider,
and will enhance either home-
made or store-purchased
preserves, such as chutneys,
mustards, ketchups or pickles.

◆■◆

THE MOUSE, THE BIRD
AND THE SAUSAGE

Making home together, the trio decided that
the Bird's work would be to fly to the forest
everyday and bring back wood; the Mouse
should carry water, make up the fire and set
the table, while the Sausage did the cooking.

PRESERVE-POT COVERS

YOU WILL NEED

For three preserve-pot covers, each measuring 18cm (7¼in) across, with a 6.5cm (2½in) central circle of evenweave Hardanger:

Three lace-edged pot covers with cream evenweave centres, 18 threads to 2.5cm (1in)
(for suppliers, see page 128)
210cm (2⅓yd) of bright pink satin ribbon, 6mm (¼in) wide
DMC stranded embroidery cotton in the colours given in the panels
No26 tapestry needle
Ribbon threader

THE EMBROIDERY

These would make lovely beginner's projects for a child wanting to learn cross stitch. So that they are easy to follow, the charts are shown to a large scale.

All three covers are worked in the same way. With the Hardanger placed centrally in a 10cm (4in) diameter hoop (see page 120), and the centre lines based both ways, you can now begin the embroidery. Following the appropriate chart, complete the cross stitching, using two strands of thread in the needle throughout. Use a single strand to work the backstitching on the mouse's body, the twigs carried by the bird and the hair and tail of the sausage.

Remove the basting stitches and steam press the finished covers on the wrong side.

Cut the ribbon into three equal lengths and, using the ribbon threader, thread it through the holes provided in the lace edging.

THE MOUSE ▶

- △ 834 yellow
- S 680 ochre
- ◆ 224 pink
- ⊡ 3772 brick red
- ◣ 800 pale blue
- I 415 grey (bks 317, including feet)
- △ 317 dark grey (bks on bird and water carriers)

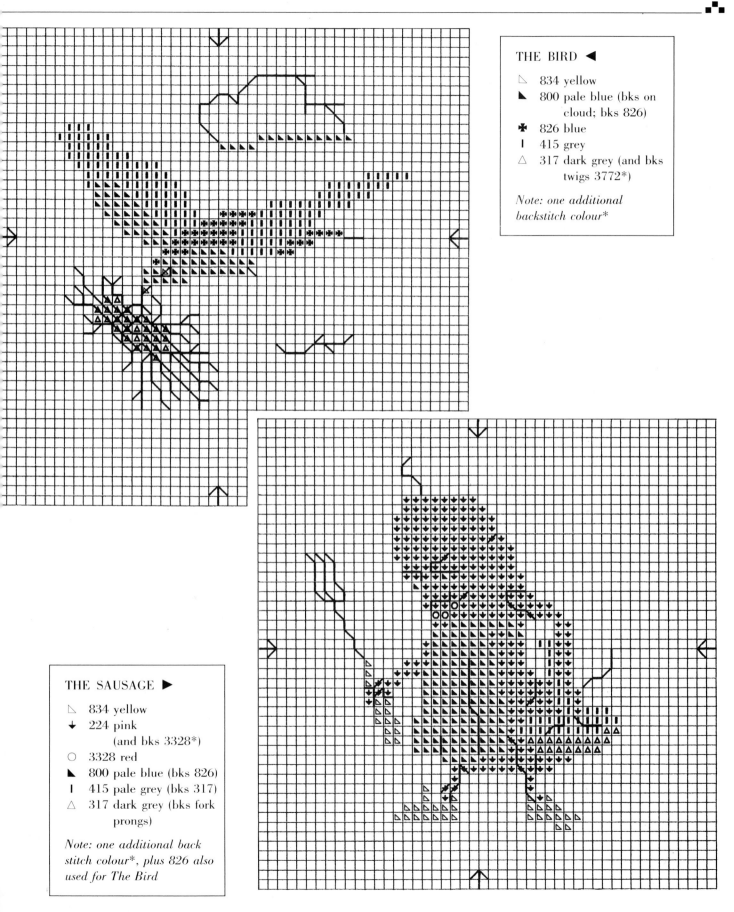

TEDDY BEAR COMPANIONS

The story of the Three Bears is the perfect choice for decorating a cushion and padded back for a child's chair. The tie-on back also has a deep pocket, large enough to hold a child's favourite possessions and several cuddly toys.

THE THREE BEARS

'Somebody has been sitting in my chair and has sat the bottom right out of it!' said the Little, Small Wee Bear, in his little, small wee voice.
'And somebody has been eating my porridge!' said the Great, Huge Bear in his great, rough gruff voice.

TEDDY BEAR COMPANIONS

YOU WILL NEED

For a chair back measuring 23cm × 20cm (9in × 8in), and a chair cushion measuring 23cm (9in) square, excluding the frills, which are 4cm (1½in) wide:

60cm (⅔yd) of pale khaki evenweave Aida fabric, 110cm (43in) wide, 16 threads to 2.5cm (1in)
30cm (12in) of matching cotton sateen, 90cm (36in) wide, for the frills
120cm (1⅓yd) of contrasting seam binding, 12mm (½in) wide
24cm × 23cm (9½in × 9in) of medium-weight synthetic batting
DMC stranded emboidery cotton in the colours given in the panels on pages 84 and 85
No26 tapestry needle
25cm (10in) square cushion pad

PREPARING THE FABRIC

Following the cutting layout, cut out the chair-back and the cushion sections from evenweave fabric. Seam allowances are included in the measurements given in the diagram.

Cut the sateen fabric into three strips across, each measuring 10cm (4in) deep, and put these to one side.

THE EMBROIDERY

Both the chair-back and the cushion are embroidered in the same way. With the fabric prepared and stretched in a frame (see page 121), centre lines basted in both directions and position line marked for the chair-back design (Back 2), begin the cross stitching.

Working with two strands of thread in the needle and following the appropriate chart, complete the embroidery. Work the backstitching last of all and note that a single strand is used for the lines on the rush seat of the chair-back design. Remove the finished embroidery from the frame and steam press it on the wrong side.

CUTTING LAYOUT

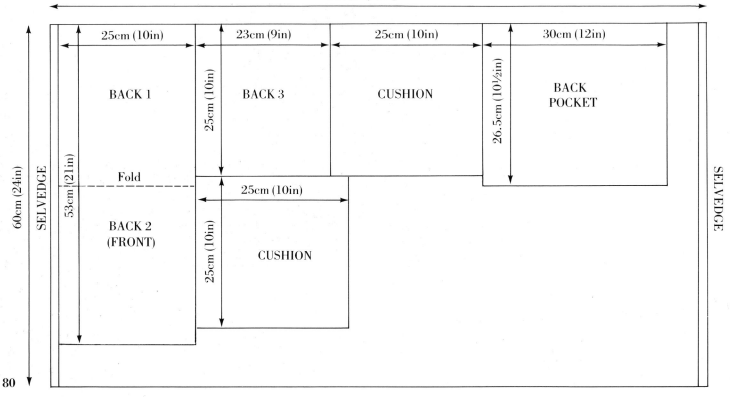

MAKING UP THE CHAIR-BACK

Using the basting lines as a guide, trim the fabric to measure 48.5cm × 23cm (19in × 9in), making sure the embroidered motif stays in the centre of the front section.

To make the frill, cut two 50cm (20in) lengths of sateen. Fold each piece lengthwise in half, right sides together, and machine stitch along the short edges. Turn through and press. Run a gathering thread along the bottom edge of each frill and pull up to measure 23cm (9in). With the right side facing, baste the frill to each long side of the front section raw edges just inside the seam allowance. Machine stitch in place.

For the ties, cut the seam binding into four equal lengths. Baste to the two short edges as shown in the diagram, so that the binding lies on the right side of the fabric and will be attached as the seams are sewn.

Place the batting on the wrong side of the lining section (Back 3), with the raw edges of three sides matching, and pin and baste it in position. Fold a single 12mm (½in) turning, enclosing the batting, at the remaining (chair top) edge of the back lining, and baste. With right sides together and the folded edge at the top (centre foldline), place the lining on the embroidered section. Stitch along the side and bottom edges. Trim the batting back and trim across the corners, then turn right side out and machine close to the fold along the top edge, stitching through all layers.

On the pocket section, machine stitch a double 12mm (½in) turning on one long edge. Make a pleat 2cm (¾in) deep at each side of the bottom edge, 6cm (2½in) in from the outer edge, and baste across.

On the main section, snip into the seam allowance on the foldline. Place the pocket section with the right side facing the wrong side of Back 1. Baste and machine stitch around three sides, leaving the top unstitched. Trim the corners and turn through to the right side. Machine stitch across the corners of the pocket top to strengthen.

MAKING UP THE CUSHION

To make the frill, join together the remaining lengths of sateen along the short edges to give a total length of 186cm (63in). Machine stitch the two

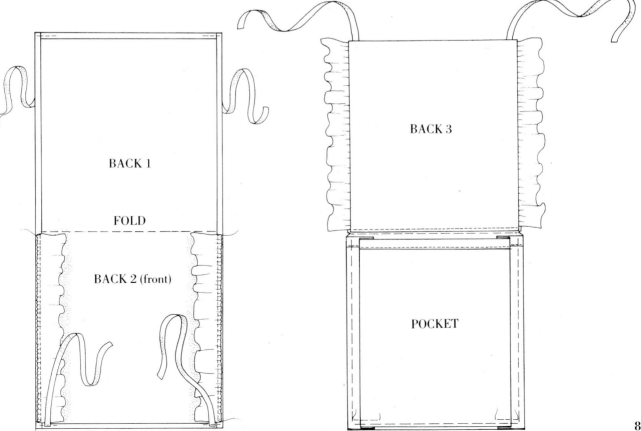

BACK 1

FOLD

BACK 2 (front)

BACK 3

POCKET

short edges together to form a circle, then turn through to the right side and press the seam open.

Fold the circular piece lengthwise in half, with wrong sides together, and press the fold. Run a gathering thread through both thicknesses along the lower edge and pull up the gathers to fit. Pin and baste to the right side of the cushion front, and stitch as for the chair-back.

Place the backing fabric and the embroidery right sides together, then baste and machine stitch around, leaving a 15cm (6in) opening in the middle of one side. Trim across the corners and turn through to the right side. Remove the basting threads and lightly press. Insert the cushion pad and slipstitch the opening to close.

To protect the finished embroidery from scuff marks and other accidents, it would be a good idea to spray it with a proprietary dirt repellant.

CUSHION ▼

‖ white	◺ 783 deep gold	I 807 turquoise	⊡ 435 light brown
⬒ 3047 cream	◆ 224 pale pink	÷ 598 blue	(bks 3781)
⊊ 676 pale yellow	● 3733 pink	↓ 523 drab green	○ 611 brown (bks 3781)
(bks claws)	◣ 504 pale turquoise	(bks on tablecloth)	✳ 3781 dark brown
	(bks 733)	△ 733 green	= 453 grey

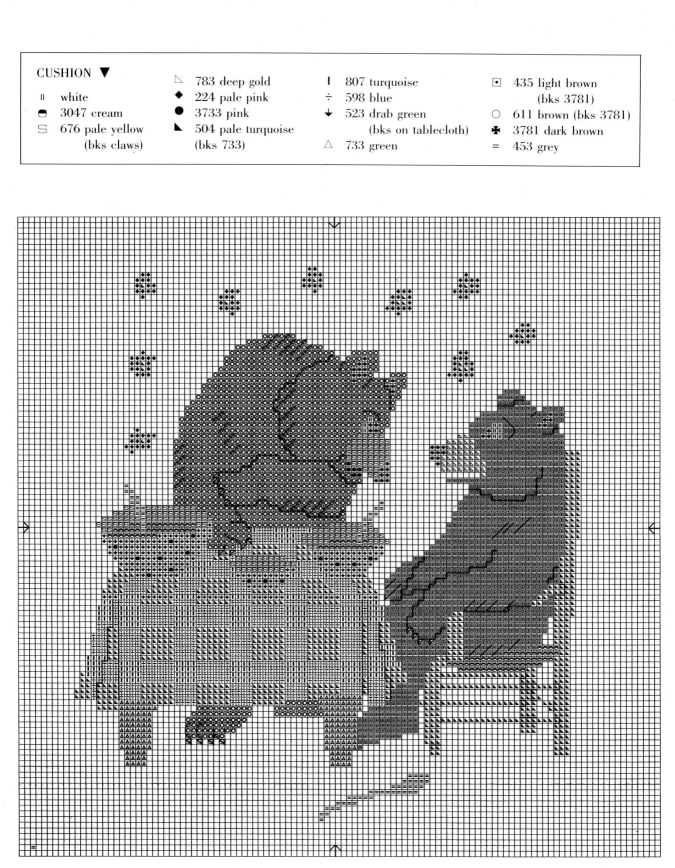

CHAIR BACK ▲

◺	white	◆	224 pale pink	✱	435 light brown
S	3047 cream (bks 783)	⊡	3733 pink (bks 504)		(horizontal bks on
I	676 pale yellow	◣	504 pale turquoise		chair front)
△	783 deep gold (bks 3781)	↓	598 blue (bks 435)	●	3781 dark brown

FRILLED BABY-BASKET COVER

This pretty and practical basket, designed to hold all baby's odds and ends, would delight any new mother. The tie-on washable cover can be removed easily for laundering – and when baby grows up you can always use the basket for toys or for family shopping. The cover is designed for a basket with a top measuring approximately 29cm × 42cm (11½in × 16½in) across, but the size can easily be adjusted.

THUMBELINA

After nursing the swallow back to health, and also to escape having to marry the mole, Thumbelina decided to fly away with the bird. 'You can sit on my back; tie yourself on with your sash and we'll fly to a warm country where it is always summer,' said the swallow.

FRILLED
BABY-BASKET COVER

YOU WILL NEED

For a cover measuring approximately
33cm × 46cm (13in × 18in) across, including a
3cm (1¼in) frill all around:

*33cm × 46cm (13in × 18in) of white evenweave
Linda fabric, or linen, 16 threads to 2.5cm (1in)
33cm × 46cm (13in × 18in) of white cotton lawn
for the lining
28cm × 40cm (11in × 16in) of medium-weight
synthetic batting
160cm (1¾yd) of white pre-gathered broderie
anglaise edging, 4cm (1½in) wide
140cm (1½yd) of white taffeta ribbon,
2.5cm (1in) wide
DMC stranded embroidery cotton in the colours
given in the panels
Matching sewing threads
Baby basket of your choice
Tracing paper*

•

PREPARING THE FABRIC

First, enlarge the graph pattern on to tracing paper
(see page 122); mark the positioning lines for the
embroidery, and cut out.

Baste the centre of the embroidery fabric both
ways; place the paper pattern on the straight grain,
matching the centre lines, and baste around the
curved edge. Repeat on the opposite side. Mark the
positioning lines for the two motifs, as shown on the
graph pattern.

Using the paper pattern, cut out the batting and
the lining fabric, adding a 12mm (½in) seam allowance all around on the lining pieces, and around
the curved edge only on the batting sections.

THE EMBROIDERY

With the prepared fabric stretched in a hoop, begin
the embroidery. Following the charts given opposite, and working with two strands of thread in the
needle, complete the cross stitching. Finish by
working the backstitch details, using a single
strand of thread.

Steam press on the wrong side. Cut out, adding
a 12mm (½in) seam allowance all round.

MAKING THE COVER

Working on the right side, baste the lace edging
around the outer edge of the embroidered section,
with the raw edge placed just inside the seam allowance, and leaving a 3cm (1¼in) space in the
middle of both long sides. This will allow the cover
to fit snugly around the basket handle, and the two
sides to be lifted independantly. Turn under the
short edges of the frill twice to neaten.

With the embroidery and the two lining sections
right sides together, place the batting on top. Baste
and machine stitch around the outer edge. Trim the
batting close to the seam, clip into the curves and
turn the cover through to the right side. Turn under
the two straight edges of the lining, unpicking a few
stiches of the outer seam as necessary, then baste
and machine stitch across.

Cut the ribbon in half and attach to each side,
stitching the centre of the ribbon over the seam
allowance in the space left, to neaten. Remove all
basting threads and lightly press to finish.

BABY BASKET COVER

1 SQUARE = 2.5cm (1in)

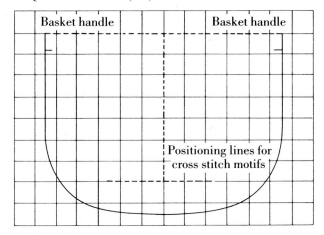

CUT TWO FROM BATTING
CUT TWO FROM LINING
Reverse on centre line and cut
one for cover top

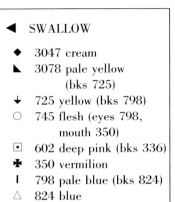

◀ SWALLOW

◆ 3047 cream

◣ 3078 pale yellow
(bks 725)

↓ 725 yellow (bks 798)

○ 745 flesh (eyes 798,
mouth 350)

⊡ 602 deep pink (bks 336)

✳ 350 vermilion

| 798 pale blue (bks 824)

△ 824 blue

● 336 dark blue

BUTTERFLY ▶

○ 3078 pale yellow
(bks inner
veins 725)

◆ 725 yellow
(bks 350)

⊡ 602 deep pink

✳ 350 vermilion

↓ 3747 pale blue

● 824 blue
(bks antennae)

△ 676 deep buff
(bks 350)

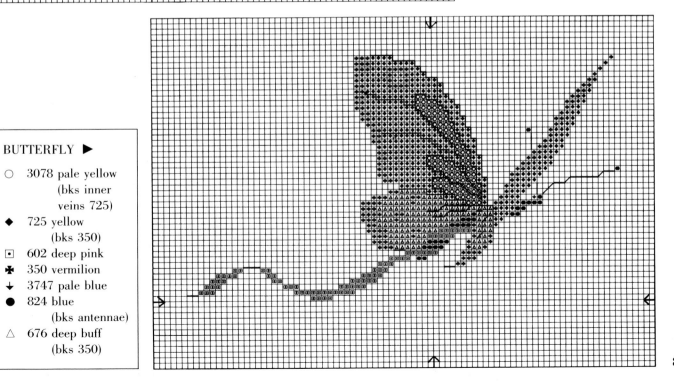

BABY'S CRIB QUILT

The ideal gift for a new baby!
Make this beautifully soft crib
quilt (or pram cover) in cotton
patchwork with cross-stitched
animal motifs taken from six of
the best-loved fairy tales.

❖

THE UGLY DUCKLING

TOM THUMB

THE HARE AND THE TORTOISE

MOTHER GOOSE

HENNY PENNY

PUSS IN BOOTS

BABY'S CRIB QUILT

YOU WILL NEED

For a quilt measuring
70.5cm × 50.5cm (28in × 20in):

*6 × 17.5cm (7in) squares of cream evenweave Aida
fabric, 14 threads to 2.5cm (1in)
90cm (36in) of pale blue lightweight cotton,
90cm (36in) wide
75cm × 52cm (29in × 21in) of medium-weight
synthetic batting
DMC stranded emboidery cotton in the colours
given in the panels on pages 96-101
No24 tapestry needle, quilting needle or betweens
Matching sewing thread
Quilting hoop, optional*

THE EMBROIDERY

Baste the centre both ways on each of the six even-weave squares, prepare the edges and stretch the first square in a hoop, see page 120. Each square includes a 12mm (½in) seam allowance all around. Following the appropriate chart, complete the embroidery, using two strands of thread in the needle throughout. Work all the cross stitching before finishing with the backstitch details.

Remove from the frame; take out the basting stitches, and steam press on the wrong side. Complete the embroidery on the five remaining squares.

MAKING UP THE QUILT

Following the cutting layout, cut out the back of the quilt and piecing strips from the contrast fabric to the sizes given. Seam allowances of 12mm (½in) are included.

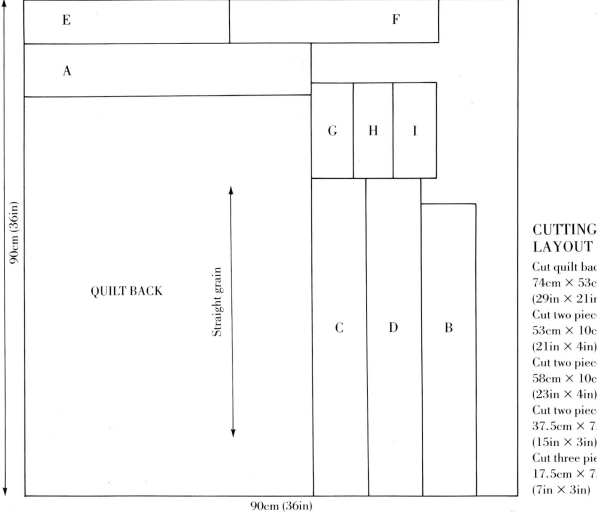

CUTTING LAYOUT

Cut quilt back
74cm × 53cm
(29in × 21in)
Cut two pieces (A, B)
53cm × 10cm
(21in × 4in)
Cut two pieces (C, D)
58cm × 10cm
(23in × 4in)
Cut two pieces (E, F)
37.5cm × 7.5cm
(15in × 3in)
Cut three pieces (G, H, I)
17.5cm × 7.5cm
(7in × 3in)

QUILT TOP

Following the position guide for the quilt top, lay out the embroidered squares in number sequence and then place the shorter contrast strips G, H and I between them to form three separate rows across. Baste and machine stitch in place, working with the evenweave on top to enable you to stitch a straight line along the grain. Press open the seams as shown in the diagram.

Join the two horizontal rows E and F in the same way. Then add the side pieces C and D, followed by A and B, to complete the quilt top.

INTERLINING

Working on a flat surface, lay the backing fabric wrong side up, place the batting on top and then the quilt top right side up. Pin the layers together and baste in several directions, starting from the middle and working outwards to the edges (see page 125).

QUILTING

With matching sewing thread in the needle (or quilting thread, which is stronger), work running stitches around each square (see page 125), placing the stitches in the seams. Make sure the needle passes through all layers and that the stitches are the same length on both sides. Should you prefer to use a quilting hoop, see also page 120. Complete the quilting.

Trim the batting around the edges to clear the seam allowance. Turn under the seams, pin, baste and, with matching thread in the needle, slipstitch around the quilt.

Remove all the basting threads and lightly press, if needed.

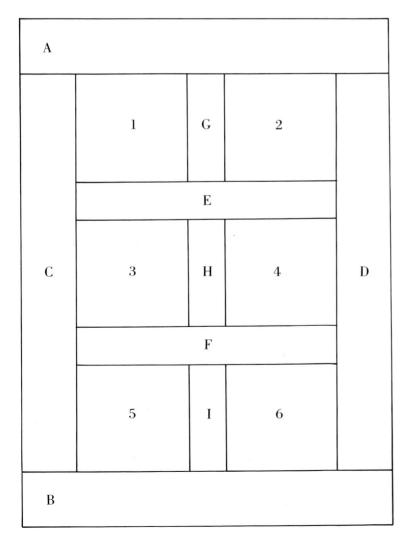

POSITION GUIDE FOR QUILT TOP

1 The Ugly Duckling
2 Tom Thumb
3 The Hare and the Tortoise
4 Mother Goose
5 Henny Penny
6 Puss in Boots

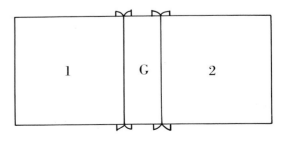

Join the horizontal rows together

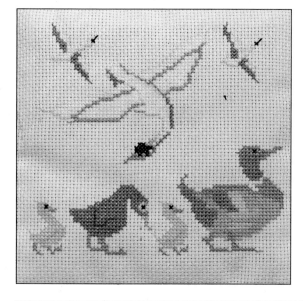

THE UGLY DUCKLING

● ■ ■ ●

Try as he might, the ugly duckling felt different and
awkward. Even while out walking, he stumbled forward
only to be jeered at by the other ducklings. Then, as tears
began to trickle down his beak, a beautiful white swan
recognized him and flew down so low she could have
touched him.

TOM THUMB

● ■ ■ ●

Crying manfully, and with great gusto, 'Shoo, shoo, crow,
shoo', Tom Thumb was helping his father to scare away
crows with a cudgell made from a barley straw. Mistaking
Tom for an ear of barley, a huge black raven suddenly
swooped down and carried him away. Tom was not
heard of again for a very long time, and his mother and
father were heartbroken.

THE HARE AND THE TORTOISE

● ■ ■ ●

Laughing at the tortoise for being so slow, the hare
challenged him to a race. As the hare was well ahead, he
thought he'd have enough time to take a nap and still win
the race. Unfortunately he slept too long and when he
woke up, the tortoise had won and called out 'I may be
slow but I always get there in the end'.

MOTHER GOOSE

In order to pay the rent, Mother goose was forced to sell her last three geese. 'Who will buy this fine laying goose?' she called. And as she spoke, a wonderful thing happened. The goose laid an egg, but this time it was not an ordinary egg but an egg of pure, shining gold.

HENNY PENNY

One day as Henny Penny was picking up corn in the rick-yard, something suddenly fell giving her an almighty whack on the head. 'Goodness gracious me!' said Henny Penny. 'The sky's going to fall! I must go at once and tell the King.' Soon she met Cocky-Locky. 'Good day, Henny Penny,' said Cocky-Locky, 'Where are you off to so early?'

PUSS IN BOOTS

With a freshly-caught brace of partridge in his bag, the Master-cat ingratiates himself to the King saying, 'My Lord Marquis sends you this tiny gift' and bows low until the feathers on his hat sweep the ground. Unaware of the plot the cat is scheming, the King eventually offers his daughter's hand to the Marquis of Carabas.

THE UGLY DUCKLING ▲

↑	white (bks 3072*)
◺	744 pale yellow
⊑	726 yellow (bks 725)
◆	725 deep yellow
	(bks 370)
△	977 orange

Ɩ	729 gold
↓	992 veridian green
◣	471 green
✳	370 light brown
	(bks 831*)
⊡	648 grey
●	3799 dark grey

Note: 831 and 3072 are used only for back-stitching here, but are also required for cross stitching on other panels.

TOM THUMB ▲

↑	744 pale yellow	⊃	754 flesh (bks 729; eye 312)
◺	725 yellow	△	603 pink
○	729 gold (bks inside barley ear)	●	309 deep pink (bks 831)
◆	733 khaki (bks whiskers on barley)	↓	794 blue (bks 312)
		✱	312 dark blue
		⊡	831 brown

HARE AND TORTOISE ▲

S	white	↓	794 blue
I	725 yellow (bks 370)	○	471 green
⊡	734 gold (bks tortoise shell 831)	△	370 light brown (bks 611*)
●	603 pink (bks 309*)	✼	831 brown

Note: 309 and 611 are used only for backstitching here, but are also required for cross stitching on other panels.

MOTHER GOOSE ▲

◣	white (bks goose front and lower wing feathers)	●	312 dark blue
I	726 yellow	↓	992 veridian green
◆	725 gold (bks straw stems)	⊡	3072 pale grey
△	977 orange (bks ears of corn)	✱	647 grey (bks upper wing feathers, beak and eye)

HENNY PENNY ▲

÷ white	I 992 veridian green
= 725 yellow	↑ 471 green (bks grass)
△ 977 orange	○ 738 fawn
✱ 350 red	⊡ 370 light brown
◣ 794 blue	● 3799 dark grey
↓ 312 dark blue (bks bird's back and head – in sky)	

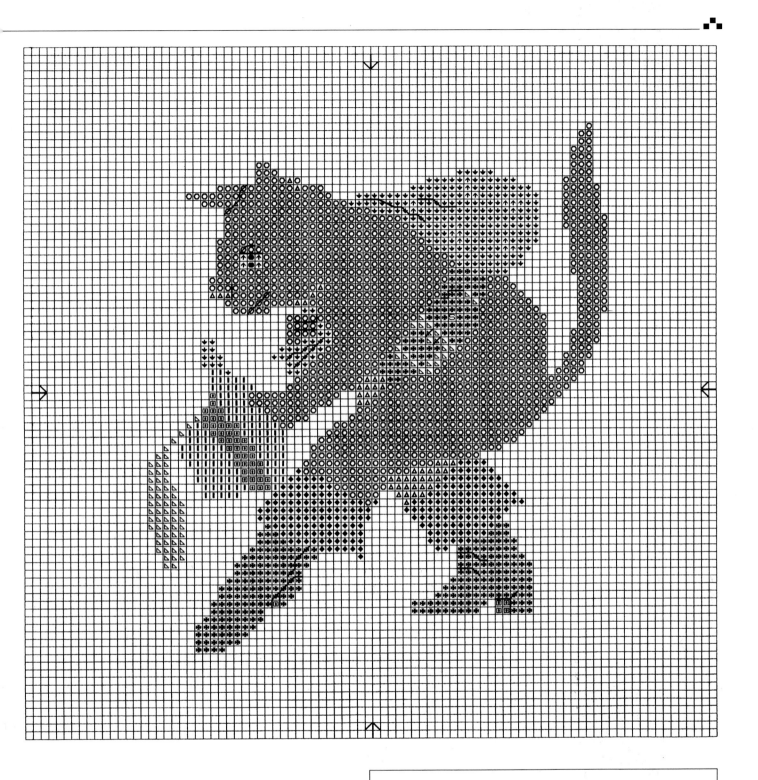

PUSS IN BOOTS ▲

↑	white
△	725 yellow
◆	603 pink
✖	309 deep pink
⊡	718 magenta
↓	794 blue (bks 792)

⊓	792 dark blue
∣	992 veridian green
○	370 light brown (bks 611)
△	611 brown
●	3799 dark grey (bks on eye)

CHRISTMAS STOCKINGS

Embroider this jolly trio of tiny
stockings ready for the children
to hang up on Christmas Eve.
They can be filled to the brim
with lots of surprise presents or,
alternatively, a single stocking
would make an original
container for an extra special gift
for someone you hold dear.

THE SNOW QUEEN

CLARA AND
THE NUTCRACKER DOLL

THE LITTLE TIN SOLDIER

CHRISTMAS STOCKINGS

YOU WILL NEED

For three stockings, each one measuring overall
23cm × 15cm (9in × 6in):

*25cm × 20cm (10in × 8in) each of cream,
red and pale blue evenweave Aida fabric,
14 threads to 2.5cm (1in)
25cm × 20cm (10in × 8in) each of cream,
red and pale blue linen backing fabric
(or contrast colours)
75cm × 20cm (30in × 8in) of lightweight
synthetic batting
75cm × 20cm (30in × 8in) of white cotton muslin
70cm (28in) each of red, royal blue and bright
yellow cotton piping
DMC stranded embroidery cotton in the colours
given in the panels on pages 105, 108 and 109
No24 tapestry needle
Matching sewing threads
Tracing paper*

•

THE EMBROIDERY

Each stocking is made in the following way. With
the edges prepared, the centre lines basted, and
your embroidery fabric stretched in a frame, see
page 121, you are ready to begin the stitchery.
Referring to the appropriate chart and colour key,
and using two strands of thread in the needle
throughout, complete the design. You will find it
easier to finish all the cross stitching first, and then
work the backstitch details on top, as instructed.
Remember when cross stitching to embroider all
the darker colours before the lighter ones.

Remove the embroidery from the frame and
steam press on the wrong side.

MAKING UP THE STOCKING

First, make a paper pattern for the stocking by
tracing the outline given with the chart on to tracing
paper. Mark the centre lines and cut out. Place the
embroidery face down and the pattern on top, then
with centre lines and basting stitches matching,

draw around the edge with a soft pencil. Working
freehand, draw a second line around, 12mm (½in)
further out. Add a further 12mm (½in) to the top
edge and cut out.

Using this section of the stocking as a template,
cut out one piece each of batting, muslin and backing fabric. Working on the right side, baste the
piping around the outer edge and machine stitch in
place using the piping foot. Use red piping for the
Tin Soldier, royal blue for Clara and the Nutcracker
Doll and yellow for The Snow Queen design.

For the loop, cut out a piece of backing fabric
measuring 13cm × 5cm (5in × 2in). Turn in the
long edges, hem in place and fold in half to form a
loop. Working on the right side, baste the loop to
the top outer edge of the stocking with the raw
edges placed at an angle (see photograph) inside
the seam line.

With the embroidery face down, place the
batting on top and then the muslin. Baste the layers
together, and treat as one layer. Place the embroidery and the backing fabric with right sides
together, baste and machine stitch around the edge,
using the piping foot, and leaving the top edge
unstitched. Trim the seam allowance to 6mm (¼in)
and clip into the curves.

On the top edge, trim back all except the top
fabrics (embroidery and backing) by 12mm (½in)
and make a double turning. Hem in place, using
matching sewing thread. Remove all basting
threads and turn the stocking to the right side.

Lightly press the stocking to finish.

ALTERNATIVE EDGING

Instead of piping, you may prefer to bind the edges
of your Christmas stockings with double-folded bias
binding in the traditional way, as shown on page 122.

In this case, hem the top edges of the stocking in
the usual way, and baste the two sections together,
with right sides outside. Pin the double-fold bias
binding over the raw edges of the stocking, starting
and finishing at the top edge. Neaten the ends of
the bias binding by turning under 6mm (¼in).

Baste and machine stitch around, stitching
through all layers. Follow the instructions for
making the loop. Turn under the raw edges and
machine stitch in place over the bound edge.

THE SNOW QUEEN ▲

● silver thread	◺ 3779 flesh (bks 224)	● 606 red (bks boy's mouth; bks 824)	= 703 green (bks 958)
÷ 726 pale yellow	↑ 778 pale dusky pink (bks 731)		◣ 958 veridian green (thorns on leaves)
S 725 yellow (bks 3045)	○ 224 dusky pink	◆ 798 blue (bks 824)	I 3045 brown
	✱ 957 rose pink	⊡ 824 dark blue	△ 731 dark brown

CLARA AND THE NUTCRACKER DOLL

Clara and the prince climbed into the boat, and off they sped through the wintry night. Snowflakes whirled around them but Clara felt as warm as if she were wrapped in a cosy eiderdown.

At last Clara and the Nutcracker prince arrived at the palace. Clara gazed at it entranced. It was made entirely from sugar, with towers of pink icing, columns of barley sugar twists and chandeliers of glistening pear-drops.

THE SNOW QUEEN

Imprisoned by the wicked Snow Queen, who had kidnapped him and carried him off to her ice palace at the north pole, Kai became cold and very unhappy. Then, after long searching, his sweetheart, Gerda, found him and wept for joy. Her warm tears melted his heart, washing away the splinter of glass from the evil mirror, and he was free. Escaping on the back of the faithful reindeer given to her by the little robber girl, they reached home by mid-summer when the sun shone and the roses were in full bloom again.

THE LITTLE TIN SOLDIER

Standing in the window on his one leg, the little tin soldier was just thinking
that the ballerina was the most beautiful doll he'd ever seen when, suddenly,
Jack jumped out of his box and the tin soldier fell through the open
window into the gutter below!

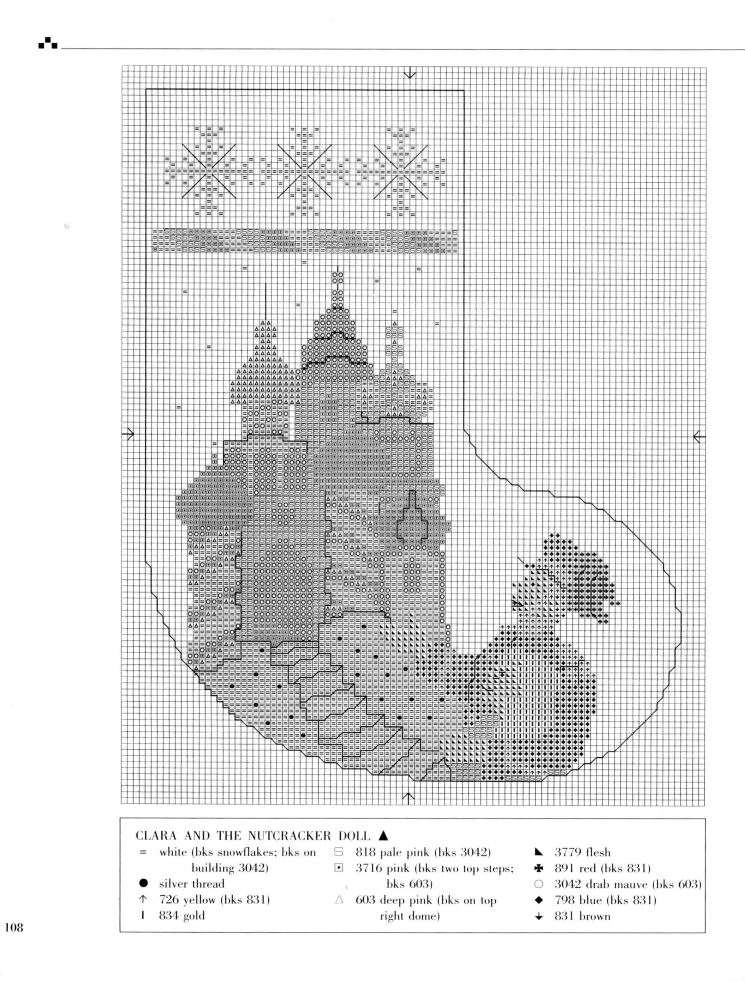

CLARA AND THE NUTCRACKER DOLL ▲

= white (bks snowflakes; bks on building 3042)	S 818 pale pink (bks 3042)	◣ 3779 flesh
● silver thread	⊡ 3716 pink (bks two top steps; bks 603)	✱ 891 red (bks 831)
↑ 726 yellow (bks 831)		○ 3042 drab mauve (bks 603)
I 834 gold	△ 603 deep pink (bks on top right dome)	◆ 798 blue (bks 831)
		↓ 831 brown

TIN SOLDIER ▲

= white	◣ 353 flesh (bks eyebrows 413)	◠ 989 green
↑ 743 yellow (and bks on toe pattern; bks 680)	✳ 3705 red (bks 413)	⊡ 370 brown (bks mouse's tail 413)
↓ 700 dark green	△ 552 purple	● 413 dark grey (and bks
○ 680 ochre (bks floor boards)	◺ 3766 turquoise (and ballerina's eye)	soldier's eye; bks 350)
	◆ 992 veridian green	

SERVING TRAY AND PICTURE

This charming design of Dick Whittington and his cat, aptly mounted in silver, would make an ideal gift for a wedding, as would the accompanying picture with its pretty portrait of Cinderella.

DICK WHITTINGTON AND HIS CAT

Before Dick could turn back, distant church bells rang out from the City of London. They seemed to be saying, 'Turn again Whittington, Lord Mayor of London.'

·

CINDERELLA

As her fairy godmother waved goodbye to Cinderella she warned, 'Remember to leave the ball before midnight, otherwise my magic will melt away.'

SERVING TRAY
AND PICTURE

YOU WILL NEED

For a tray 23cm (9in) in diameter:
*30cm (12in) square of cream evenweave Aida
fabric, 14 threads to 2.5cm (1in)
DMC stranded emboidery cotton in the colours
given in the panel
No24 tapestry needle
Silver-plated tray (for suppliers, see page 128)*

For a miniature picture 15cm (6in) in diameter:
*21cm (8¼in) square of cream Hardanger
18 threads to 2.5cm (1in)
DMC stranded embroidery cotton in the colours
given in the panel
No26 tapestry needle
Picture frame (for suppliers, see page 128)*

THE EMBROIDERY

Both the tray and the picture are worked in the
following way.

Prepare the fabric, and stretch it in a frame or
hoop, see the instructions on pages 120 and 121.
Referring to the appropriate chart, complete the
cross stitching.

For each embroidery, use two strands of thread
in the needle throughout, with the exception of the
backstitch details on the Cinderella design, which
are worked with a single strand.

Steam press the finished embroidery on the
wrong side.

ASSEMBLING THE TRAY
AND THE MINIATURE PICTURE

In each case, stretch the embroidery over the card
mount supplied, following the instructions given for
the Miniature Pictures on page 52.

Complete the assembly, following the manufacturer's instructions.

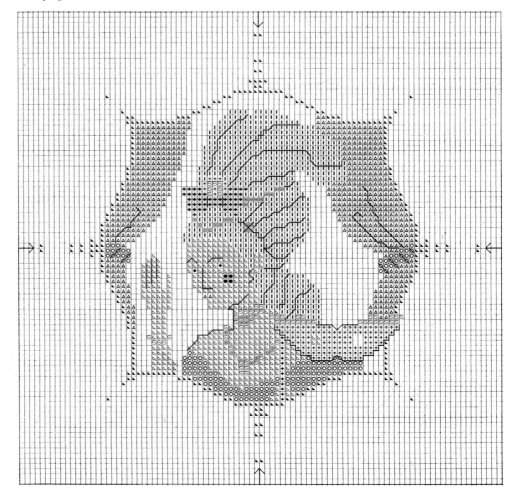

◀ CINDERELLA

↑ 3078 pale yellow (bks 744)

S 744 yellow

◣ 834 gold

◺ 818 pale pink (bks 3354)

● 3716 pink

⊡ 3731 deep pink (bks on tiebacks)

△ 3354 deep dusky pink (bks 3041)

○ 3743 drab mauve

✱ 3041 purple

◆ 341 blue

I 762 grey (bks hair 381; bks feathers 341)

↓ 318 dark grey

DICK WHITTINGTON ▲

‖ white

÷ 726 yellow

☻ 834 gold

I 680 ochre (bks 434)

◺ 951 flesh (bks 680)

● 606 red (bks stockings 319*; bks hat 434)

= 828 pale blue (bks 799)

↓ 799 blue

↑ 3347 green

○ 3052 drab green (bks stems)

△ 434 brown (bks cat front)

✱ 610 dark brown (bks whiskers and cat's legs)

◆ 928 light grey

⊡ 927 grey

*Note: one additional backstitch colour**

ALPHABETS AND NUMBERS

Elegant and graceful, simple or decorative, upright or sloping – cross-stitch alphabets and numbers can be as varied as you like. You can mix capital letters with lower case letters to spell out names, quotations and phrases, and add commemorative dates to give a very special piece of embroidery a truly personal touch.

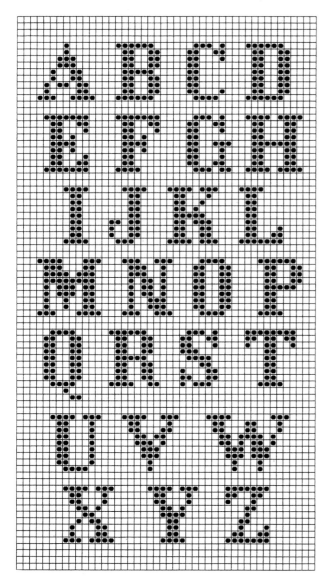

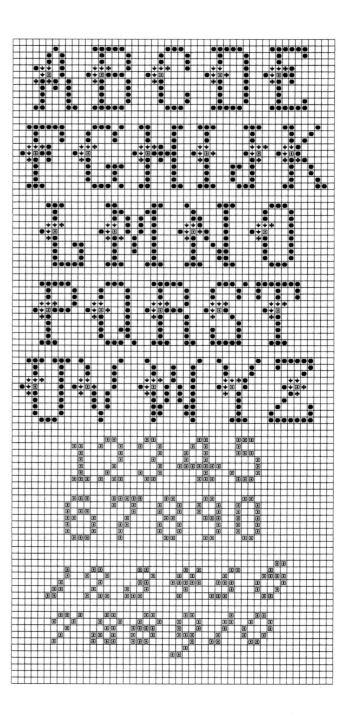

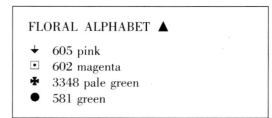

FLORAL ALPHABET ▲

- ↓ 605 pink
- ▫ 602 magenta
- ✳ 3348 pale green
- ● 581 green

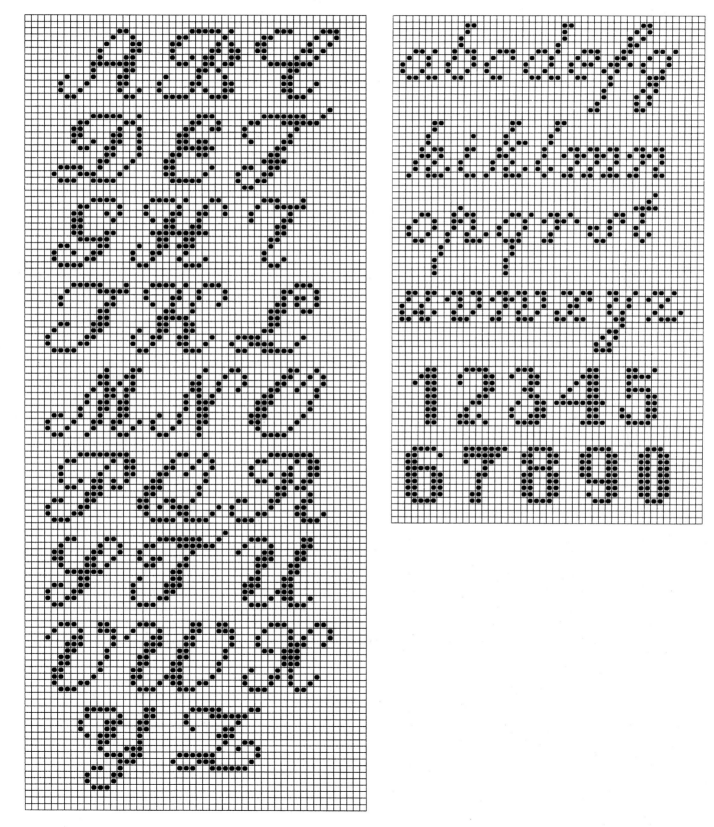

BORDERS

Even the simplest of borders, perhaps worked around either a cushion or a picture, will give a sense of completeness to the embroidery. Choosing the right one can be fun, but if you are not sure which to select, then photocopy the page, cut out a varied range, and try them on your embroidery – placing them at varying intervals away from your embroidery until you arrive at a pleasing balance, and then cross stitching in matching or toning colours.

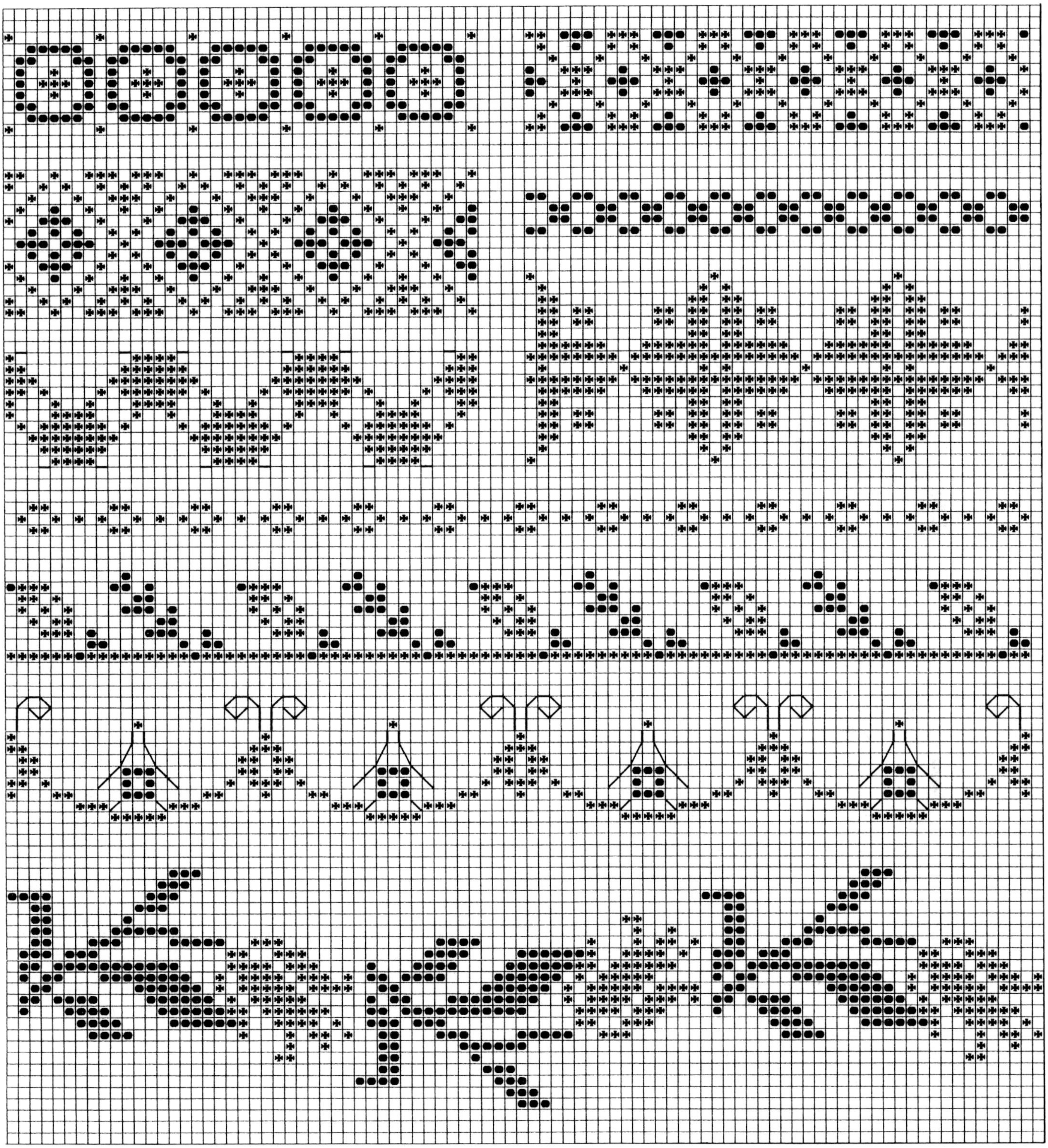

CORNERS

A well-chosen corner motif, perhaps placed at the top and bottom of a narrow sampler, or surrounding a central motif on a cushion, for example, could be used to expand a design, while giving a sense of balance and finish to the embroidery. A triangular corner (such as any of those shown below), repeated symmetrically around a central motif, can be linked by one or more lines of cross stitching, so that the four linked corners combine to create a contrasting and pleasing geometric border around the motif.

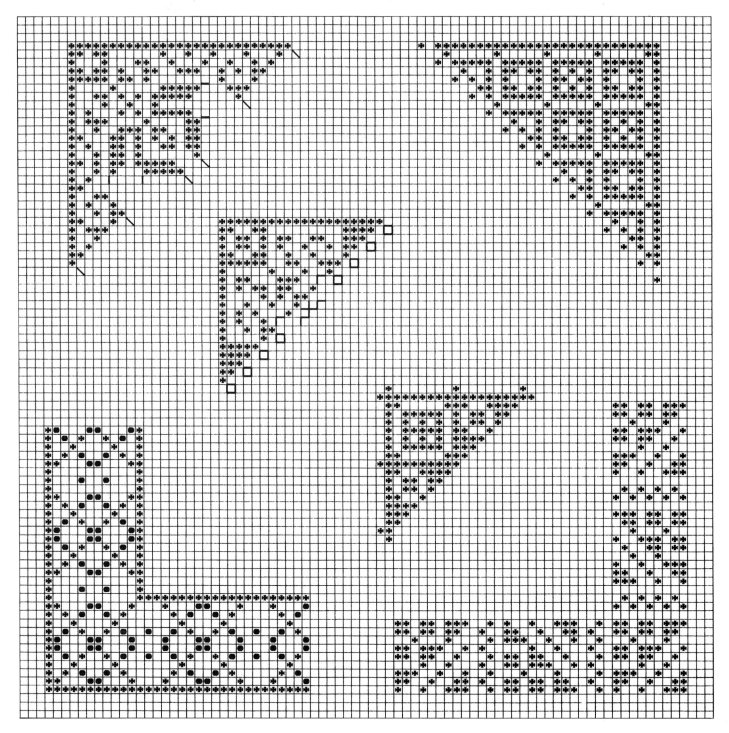

BASIC EQUIPMENT

The basic equipment needed for cross stitching is moderately simple and can be bought at most department stores or needlework suppliers. In fact, when you begin to collect the items together, you will probably find that you already have most of them in your workbox and around the home.

FABRICS

For best results, cross stitch is worked on an evenweave fabric – one with the same number of threads counted in both directions over, for example, 2.5cm (1in). Traditionally, cross stitch embroidery is worked on linen, which often has a charming hand-woven finish. Although they are not now produced in the variety and quantities of former years, linens in a limited range of weights and colours – including Hardanger and huckaback – can be brought from specialist suppliers. Whereas ordinary linens have a single weave, Hardanger has a double weave, and huckaback is woven in groups of threads to form a checked pattern.

In addition to linens, many other evenweaves are available; some of these, such as Zweigart's Quaker cloth, are cotton and linen mixes, while others are made by pure cotton, or cotton/synthetic mixes. The last include Zweigart's Aida and Tula, which are also woven with groups of threads and have a pronounced checked effect. They are produced in different weights and many colours. Zweigart's Ainring, Lugana and Linda have a single weave and are also available in a range of weights and colours.

Aida and some other cotton fabrics can be quite stiff to handle, due to the fact that they are finished with a fairly heavy dressing. This will wash out to a certain extent, and although the stiffened fabric will help to give the embroidery an even tension, you may prefer to hand wash the fabric beforehand.

THREADS

Different types of thread can be used for cross stitch embroidery but, for the purposes of this book, stranded embroidery cotton has been used throughout. The number of strands required for each project is given with the instructions.

As a general rule, however, the thickness of the embroidery thread should match the weight of the fabric. And for best results, the aim should be to have clearly defined stitches which cover the fabric well and give a sharpness to the overall design.

NEEDLES

For cross stitching on evenweave fabric, use round-ended tapestry needles. You will find that these move easily between the intersections of the fabric without piercing the ground threads. Tapestry needles are available in sizes ranging from 18–26.

When finishing the projects, a selection of sharps is required for hand sewing, and for quilting, either quilting needles or betweens are recommended.

FRAMES

Depending on the size of the embroidery and the amount of cross stitching involved, either a rectangular frame or a hoop of the appropriate size can be used to support the fabric while stitching.

Although a frame is not an absolute essential, there are positive advantages to using one. Firstly, it will keep the fabric evenly stretched and prevent it from becoming distorted. This can easily happen when working with fabric in the hand, especially if the stitch is made by 'scooping' the fabric.

Secondly, if the frame is supported, both hands are free to stitch. With one hand on top and the other below, the correct up and down movements can be used – and with practice, you will find that you can work quicker this way.

SCISSORS

In all fabric crafts it is essential to keep the right type of scissors for the job. For cutting out, use sharp dressmaker's shears and, to prevent the blades from becoming blunt, do not allow them to be used for other tasks. For snipping into seams and cutting threads, a pair of sharp-pointed small embroidery scissors are needed. It is also a good idea to have a pair of general-purpose scissors for cutting paper, card, cord and so on.

SEWING MACHINE

A sewing machine should be used for all making-up purposes where seaming is involved, especially on large items such as quilts and cushion covers. You will not need an elaborate machine to make up the projects in this book. All that is required is that it stitches reliably, gives a good straight stitch and, ideally, has a reverse stitch for starting and finishing.

IRON

This is one of the most important pieces of equipment required for any fabric craft. A thermostatically controlled steam iron gives excellent results and is particularly good for this type of embroidery, for pressing seams, and for general ironing.

When making up projects, always keep your iron and board to hand so that you can 'press as you sew' to get the very best finish.

GENERAL ACCESSORIES

In addition to the items already mentioned; you will require a good supply of dressmaker's stainless steel pins, a measuring tape, basting thread, tracing paper, ruler and pencil.

While a thimble is not necessarily used for embroidery, it is a good idea to use one for general sewing purposes, especially for hand-sewing through bulky seams. For all kinds of quilting, you will find that one, if not two, thimbles are essential. Here, the second thimble is worn on the first or second finger of the hand below the frame as it guides the needle back through the fabric.

$\mathcal{B}$ASIC SKILLS

The basic skills required for making the projects in the book can be found in the following pages.

PREPARING THE FABRIC

Unless fabrics have been stored unfolded on a roll, they will probably be creased, especially along the centre. Before cutting out, therefore, steam press all fabrics to remove any creases. When cutting out main sections, try to be as economical as possible, cutting on the grainline to avoid waste.

Even with an average amount of handling, many evenweave fabrics tend to fray at the edges, so it is a good idea to overcast the raw edges, using ordinary sewing thread, before you begin the embroidery.

WORKING IN A HOOP

A hoop is the most popular frame for use with small areas of embroidery. It consists of two rings, one fitted inside the other; the outer ring usually has an adjustable screw attachment so that it can be tightened to hold the stretched fabric in place. Hoops are available in several sizes, ranging from 10cm (4in) in diameter to quilting hoops with a diameter of 38cm (15in). Hoops with table stands or floor stands attached are also available.

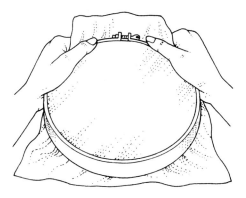

1 To stretch your fabric in a hoop, place the area to be embroidered over the inner ring and press the outer ring over it with the tension screw released.

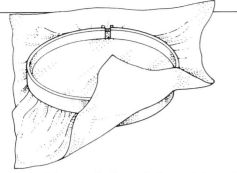

2 Smooth the fabric and, if needed, straighten the grain before tightening the screw. The fabric should be evenly stretched.

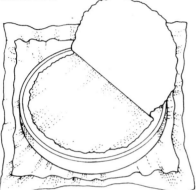

● Tissue paper can be placed between the outer ring and the embroidery, so that the hoop does not mark the fabric. Tear away the paper as shown in the diagram.

EXTENDING EMBROIDERY FABRIC

It is easy to extend a piece of embroidery fabric, such as a bookmark, to stretch it in a hoop.

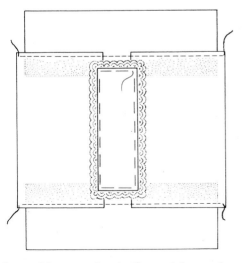

● Fabric oddments of a similar weight can be used. Simply cut four pieces to size (in other words, to the measurement that will fit both the embroidery fabric and your hoop) and baste them to each side

of the embroidery fabric before stretching it in the hoop in the usual way.

WORKING IN A RECTANGULAR FRAME

Rectangular frames are more suitable for larger pieces of embroidery. They consist of two rollers, with tapes attached, and two flat side pieces, which slot into the rollers and are held in place by pegs or screw attachments. Available in different sizes, either alone or with adjustable table or floor stands, frames are measured by the length of the roller tape, and range in size from 30cm (12in) to 68cm (27in).

As alternatives to a slate frame, canvas stretchers and the backs of old picture frames can be used. Provided there is sufficient extra fabric around the finished size of the embroidery, the edges can be turned under and simply attached with drawing pins (thumb tacks) or staples.

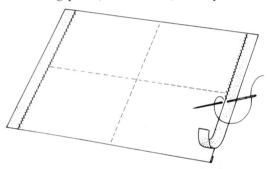

1 To stretch your fabric in a rectangular frame, cut out the fabric, allowing at least an extra 5cm (2in) all around the finished size of the embroidery. Baste a single 12mm (½in) turning on the top and bottom edges and oversew strong tape, 2.5cm (1in) wide, to the other two sides. Mark the centre line both ways with basting stitches.

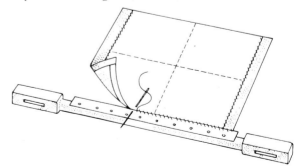

2 Working from the centre outwards and using strong thread, oversew the top and bottom edges to the roller tapes. Fit the side pieces into the slots, and roll any extra fabric on one roller until the fabric is taut.

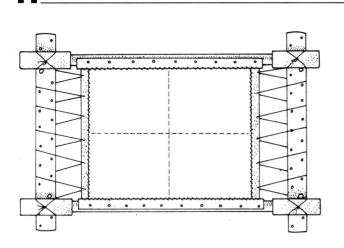

3 Insert the pegs or adjust the screw attachments to secure the frame. Thread a large-eyed needle (chenille needle) with strong thread or fine string and lace both edges, securing the ends around the intersections of the frame. Lace the webbing at 2.5cm (1in) intervals, stretching the fabric evenly.

ENLARGING A GRAPH PATTERN

One or two graph patterns are given in this book. These must be enlarged to the correct size. The scale of the full-size pattern is given on the page; for example, 'Each square = 5cm (2in)' means that each small square on the printed diagram corresponds to a 5cm (2in) square on your enlarged grid.

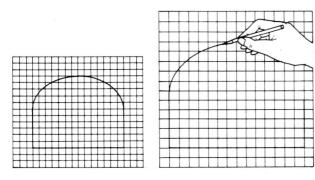

● To enlarge a graph pattern, you will need a sheet of graph paper ruled in 1cm (⅜in) squares, a ruler and pencil. If, for example, the scale is one square to 5cm (2in) you should first mark the appropriate lines to give a grid of the correct size. Copy the graph freehand from the small grid to the larger one, completing one square at a time. Use a ruler to draw the straight lines first, and then copy the freehand curves.

BIAS BINDING

As its name suggests, bias binding is cut across the grain to allow maximum 'give', and is an excellent binding for all edges, especially curves.

It is available in three sizes – 12mm (½in), 2.5cm (1in) and 5cm (2in) – and in a wonderful variety of colours. Cotton lawn is by far the most popular and practical type, although satins and synthetic mixes are also available. Two methods of binding an edge are shown here; in the first, the binding is attached by stitching through all layers, while in the second, it is attached in two stages, so that the stitching cannot be seen on the right side.

TO BIND AN EDGE

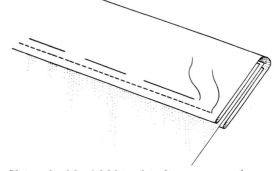

● Using double-fold bias binding, encase the raw edge with binding and baste in place. Working from the right side, machine stitch along the edge so that both sides are stitched at the same time.

ALTERNATIVE BINDING METHOD

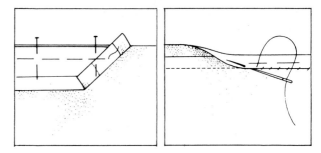

1 Open out the turning on one edge of the binding and pin in position on the right side of the fabric, matching the fold to the seamline. Fold over the cut end of the binding. Finish by overlapping the starting point by about 12mm (½in). Baste and machine stitch along the seamline.

2 Fold the binding over the raw edge to the wrong side, baste and, using matching sewing thread, neatly hem to finish.

PIPED SEAMS

Contrasting piping adds a special decorative finish to a seam and looks particularly attractive on items such as cushions and cosies.

You can cover piping cord with either bias-cut fabric of your choice or a bias binding; alternatively, ready-covered piping cord is available in several widths and many colours.

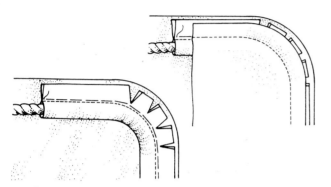

1 To apply piping, pin and baste it to the right side of the fabric, with seam lines matching. Clip into the seam allowance where necessary.

2 With right sides together, place the second piece of fabric on top, enclosing the piping. Baste and then either hand stitch in place or machine stitch, using a zipper foot. Stitch as close to the piping as possible, covering the first line of stitching.

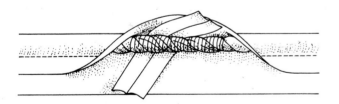

3 To join ends of piping cord together, first overlap the two ends by about 2.5cm (1in). Unpick the two cut ends of bias to reveal the cord. Join the bias strip as shown. Trim and press the seam open. Unravel and splice the two ends of the cord. Fold the bias strip over it, and finish basting around the edge.

MOUNTING EMBROIDERY

Embroidered pictures and other similar projects look best if they are first stretched over cardboard before framing. Very lightweight fabrics can be attached at the back with pieces of masking tape, but heavier fabrics are best laced across the back.

The cardboard should be cut to the size of the finished embroidery, with an extra 6mm (¼in) added all around to allow for the recess in the picture frame.

LIGHTWEIGHT FABRICS

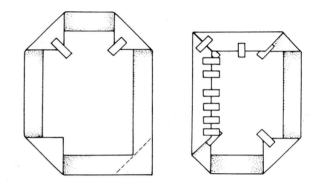

1 Place the emboidery face down, with the cardboard centred on top, and basting and pencil lines matching. Begin by folding over the fabric at each corner and securing it with small pieces of masking tape.

2 Working first on one side and then the other, fold over the fabric on all sides and secure it firmly with pieces of masking tape, placed about 2.5cm (1in) apart. Also neaten the mitred corners with masking tape, pulling the fabric tightly to give a firm, smooth finish.

HEAVIER FABRICS

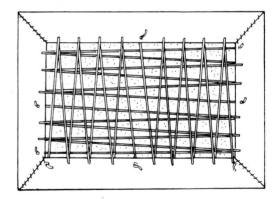

● Lay embroidery face down, with the cardboard centred on top; fold over the edges of the fabric on opposite sides, making mitred folds at the corners, and lace across, using strong thread. Repeat on the other two sides. Finally, pull up the stitches fairly tightly to stretch the fabric firmly over the cardboard. Overstitch the mitred corners.

CROSS STITCH

For all cross stitch embroidery, the following two methods of working are used. In each case, neat rows of vertical stitches are produced on the back of the fabric.

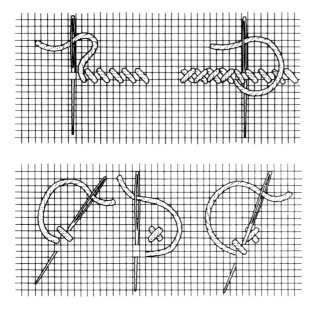

● When stitching large areas, work in horizontal rows. Working from right to left, complete the first row of evenly spaced diagonal stitches over the number of threads specified in the project instructions. Then, working from left to right, repeat the process. Continue in this way, making sure each stitch crosses in the same direction throughout.

● When stitching diagonal lines, work downwards, completing each stitch before moving to the next one.

HEMSTITCH

This stitch is the traditional way of finishing the hems of embroidered napkins and tablecloths. For a fringed hem, remove a single thread at the hem and stitch along the line as shown. When you have finished, remove the weft threads below the hemstitching, to make the fringe.

Note When hemstitching Aida and similar fabrics, it is not necessary to remove the initial thread; the stitches can be worked along a line of 'blocks' or groups of threads. As you are stitching blocks instead of single threads, make sure that you refer

to the project instructions to discover the number of blocks to work for the hemstitching.

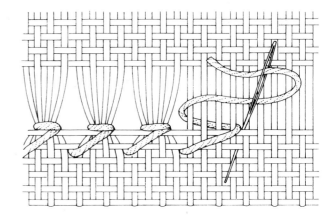

● Bring the needle out on the right side, two threads below the drawn-thread line. Working from left to right, pick up either two or three threads, as shown in the diagram. Bring the needle out again and insert it behind the fabric, to emerge two threads down, ready to make the next stitch. Before reinserting the needle, pull the thread tight, so that the bound threads form a neat group.

BACKSTITCH

Backstitch is used in the projects to give emphasis to a particular foldline, an outline or a shadow. The stitches are worked over the same number of threads as the cross stitch, forming continuous straight or diagonal lines.

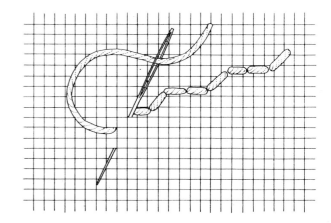

● Make the first stitch from left to right; pass the needle behind the fabric, and bring it out one stitch length ahead to the left. Repeat and continue in this way along the line.

STITCHING ON BEADS

Use the same method to attach small, even-shaped beads and pearls.

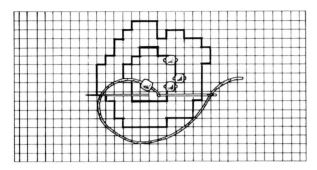

● Using either a fine crewel needle, number 9 or 10, or a beading straw for very fine beads, and sewing thread or fine silk, bring out the needle and thread on a bead. Reinsert the needle through the same hole, then make a stitch the width of the bead (and in this case, the width of the cross stitch), and pull through, with the thread below the needle. Repeat, completing the design as instructed.

QUILTING

In patchwork quilt-making (see the Baby's Crib Quilt, page 90) a soft layer of batting is inserted between two outer layers, and the layers are held in place by quilting stitches. These are worked around each geometric shape, the stitches being placed either directly in the seam or just outside.

BASTING THE LAYERS TOGETHER

Lay the backing fabric wrong side up on a flat surface. Place the batting on top and then the quilt top, right side up. Pin the layers together in the centre and along the edges. With a long length of thread, baste diagonal lines across the quilt.
● Baste vertically and horizontally, as shown in the diagram. Basting in this way helps to keep the

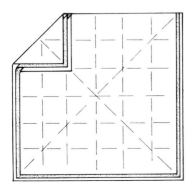

fabric even, and prevents unwanted fullness from building up in the centre.

HAND QUILTING

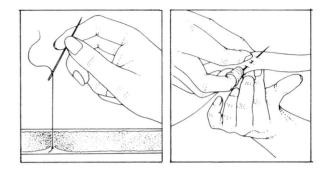

1 Working in a hoop will keep your fabric evenly stretched and give a pleasant puffed effect to the finished quilting. Using a quilting needle and a fairly short length of quilting thread, knot the end. Pull the knot through the backing fabric and into the batting.

2 With a thimble on the second finger of the sewing hand, make several stitches. Keep your thumb pressed down on the fabric, just ahead of the needle, while the hand below, also with a thimble on the first or second finger, feels the needle and guides it back through the layers.

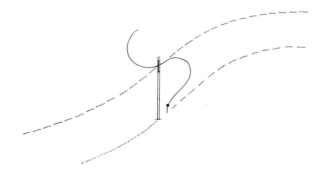

3 Finish off with a couple of back stitches or make a knot close to the last stitch and take the thread through to the back. Pull the knot through into the batting and cut the thread.

CONVERSION CHART

Not all of these colour conversions are exact matches, and bracketed
numbers are given as close substitutes.

DMC	ANCHOR	COATS	MADEIRA	DMC	ANCHOR	COATS	MADEIRA	DMC	ANCHOR	COATS	MADEIRA
White	2	1001	White	434	309	5000	2009	721	(324)	2329	0308
208	(110)	4301	0804	435	(365)	5371	2010	722	(323)	2099	0307
209	105	4302	0803	436	(363)	5943	2011	725	(306)	2298	0108
210	104	4303	0802	437	362	5942	2012	726	295	2294	0109
213	895	—	0812	444	291	2298	0108	727	293	—	0110
221	(897)	3242	0811	445	288	—	0103	734	(279)	—	1610
224	893	3241	0813	469	267	—	1503	738	942	5375	2013
225	892	3006	0814	471	(280)	—	1501	739	(366)	5369	2014
300	(352)	—	2304	498	(47)	—	0511	740	316	2099	0202
301	(349)	—	2306	517	(162)	—	1107	741	304	2314	0201
304	(47)	3401	0509	535	(401)	8400	1809	742	303	2303	0114
307	(289)	2290	0104	550	(101)	4107	0714	743	(297)	2302	0113
309	(42)	3284	0507	552	100	4092	0713	744	(301)	2293	0112
310	403	8403	Black	553	98	4097	0712	745	(300)	2296	0111
311	148	—	1006	554	(96)	4104	0711	746	(386)	—	0101
312	(147)	7979	1005	564	203	—	1208	754	(6)	2331	0305
317	(400)	8512	1714	597	(168)	—	1110	758	868	2337	0403
318	(399)	8511	1802	602	(63)	3063	0702	760	(9)	3069	0405
319	(246)	6246	1313	603	(62)	3001	0701	761	(8)	3068	0404
320	(216)	6017	1311	605	(50)	3151	0613	762	397	8510	1804
321	47	3500	0510	606	335	2334	0209	772	(264)	6250	1604
322	(978)	7978	1004	608	(333)	2332	0206	776	(24)	3281	0503
326	(59)	3401	0508	610	906	—	2106	778	(968)	—	0808
333	119	—	0903	611	898	—	2107	780	309	—	2214
334	161	7977	1003	612	832	—	2108	781	308	—	2213
335	(42)	3283	0506	613	831	—	2109	782	307	—	2212
340	118	7110	0902	632	(936)	—	2311	783	307	—	2211
341	117	—	0901	640	903	5393	1905	791	941	—	0904
347	(19)	3013	0407	642	392	—	1906	792	941	7150	0905
349	13	2335	0212	644	830	8501	1907	793	121	721	0906
350	(11)	3011	0213	645	(400)	8500	1811	794	120	—	0907
351	(10)	3012	0214	647	(8581)	8900	1813	796	(133)	7100	0913
352	(9)	3008	0303	648	900	8390	1814	797	(132)	7023	0912
353	(8)	3006	0304	666	46	3046	0210	798	(131)	7022	0911
355	5968	2339	0401	676	891	2305	2208	799	(130)	7030	0910
367	(262)	6018	1312	677	(886)	2300	2207	800	(128)	—	0908
368	(261)	6016	1310	680	901	5374	2210	801	(357)	5475	2007
371	(856)	—	2111	699	(923)	6228	1303	806	(169)	—	1108
402	(347)	—	2307	700	229	6227	1304	807	(168)	—	1109
407	(882)	—	2310	701	227	6226	1305	809	(130)	7021	0909
413	401	8514	1713	702	226	6239	1306	813	(160)	—	1013
414	(400)	8513	1801	703	238	6238	1307	814	(44)	—	0514
415	398	8510	1803	704	(256)	6238	1308	815	43	3000	0513
420	(375)	5374	2104	712	(387)	5387	2101	816	(20)	3410	0512
422	(373)	5372	2102	718	88	—	0707	817	47	2335	0211
433	(371)	5471	2008	720	(326)	—	0309	818	48	3281	0502

DMC	ANCHOR	COATS	MADEIRA	DMC	ANCHOR	COATS	MADEIRA	DMC	ANCHOR	COATS	MADEIRA
819	(892)	3280	0501	943	188	—	1203	3078	292	2292	0102
822	(390)	5387	1908	945	881	—	2313	3325	(159)	7976	1002
823	150	—	1008	946	332	—	0207	3326	(26)	3126	0504
824	(164)	—	1010	947	(330)	2327	0205	3328	(11)	3071	0408
825	(162)	—	1011	948	(778)	2331	0306	3345	(268)	6258	1406
826	(161)	—	1012	950	4146	—	2309	3346	(257)	6258	1407
827	(159)	—	1014	951	(880)	—	2308	3347	(267)	6266	1408
828	(158)	—	1101	954	204	—	1211	3348	265	6266	1409
829	(906)	—	2113	955	203	—	1210	3350	69	—	0603
833	907	—	2114	956	54	—	0611	3354	(75)	—	0608
834	874	—	2204	957	52	—	0612	3364	(843)	6010	1603
838	380	7982	1914	958	187	6186	1114	3371	382	—	2004
840	(379)	5379	1912	959	186	6185	1113	3607	(87)	—	0708
841	(378)	5376	1911	961	40	—	0610	3608	86	—	0709
842	376	—	1910	962	52	—	0609	3609	(85)	—	0710
844	401	—	1810	963	48	—	0608	3685	(70)	—	0602
869	(944)	—	2105	966	206	—	1209	3687	(68)	—	0604
890	(218)	6021	1314	970	(316)	2327	0204	3688	(66)	—	0605
891	29	—	0411	971	(316)	2099	0203	3689	73	—	0607
892	28	—	0412	972	303	—	0107	3705	(35)	—	0410
893	27	—	0413	973	297	—	0105	3706	(33)	—	0409
894	26	—	0414	975	352	—	2303	3708	(31)	—	0408
898	360	5476	2006	976	(309)	—	2302	3712	10	—	—
899	(27)	3282	0505	977	(307)	2306	2301	3731	76	—	—
902	(72)	3083	0601	986	(246)	6021	1404	3733	75	—	—
904	(258)	6258	1413	987	(245)	6258	1403	3756	158	—	—
906	(256)	6256	1411	988	(257)	6258	1402	3761	159	—	—
910	(228)	6031	1301	989	(256)	6266	1401	3766	167	—	—
911	(205)	6205	1214	991	212	—	1204	3774	778	—	—
912	209	6225	1212	992	(187)	6186	1202	3779	4146	—	—
919	(341)	2326	0314	993	(186)	—	1201				
920	(339)	3337	0312	995	410	7010	1102				
921	(338)	2326	0311	996	433	7001	1103				
922	(324)	3336	0310	3011	856	—	1607				
924	(851)	6008	1706	3021	(382)	5395	1904				
926	(779)	6007	1707	3022	(8581)	—	1903				
927	(849)	6006	1708	3024	(391)	8390	1901				
928	(900)	7225	1709	3031	(905)	5472	2003				
930	(922)	7052	1712	3033	387	—	2001				
931	(921)	7051	1711	3042	869	4221	0807				
932	(920)	7050	1710	3045	(888)	—	2103				
935	862	—	1505	3046	(887)	2410	2206				
936	269	—	1507	3047	(886)	2300	2205				
937	268	—	1504	3051	(846)	—	1508				
938	381	—	2005	3052	(844)	—	1509				
939	152	—	1009	3053	(859)	6315	1510				

INDEX

SUPPLIERS

The following mail order company has supplied some of the basic items needed for making up the projects in this book:

Framecraft Miniatures Limited
148-150 High Street
Aston
Birmingham, B6 4US
England
Telephone (021) 359 4442

Addresses for Framecraft worldwide
Ireland Needlecraft Pty. Ltd.
2-4 Keppel Drive
Hallam, Victoria 3803
Australia

Danish Art Needlework
PO Box 442, Lethbridge
Alberta T1J 3Z1
Canada

Sanyei Imports
PO Box 5, Hashima Shi
Gifu 501-62
Japan

The Embroidery Shop
286 Queen Street
Masterton
New Zealand

Anne Brinkley Designs Inc.
246 Walnut Street
Newton
Mass. 02160
USA

S A Threads and Cottons Ltd.
43 Somerset Road
Cape Town
South Africa

For information on your nearest stockist of embroidery cotton, contact the following:

DMC

UK
DMC Creative World Limited
62 Pullman Road
Wigston
Leicester, LE8 2DY
Telephone: 0533 811040

USA
The DMC Corporation
Port Kearney Bld.
10 South Kearney
N.J. 07032-0650
Telephone: 201 589 0606

AUSTRALIA
DMC Needlecraft Pty
P.O. Box 317
Earlswood 2206
NSW 2204
Telephone: 02599 3088

COATS AND ANCHOR

UK
Kilncraigs Mill
Alloa
Clackmannanshire
Scotland, FK10 1EG
Telephone: 0259 723431

USA
Coats & Clark
P.O. Box 27067
Dept CO1
Greenville
SC 29616
Telephone: 803 234 0103

AUSTRALIA
Coats Patons Crafts
Thistle Street
Launceston
Tasmania 7250
Telephone: 00344 4222

MADEIRA

UK
Madeira Threads (UK) Limited
Thirsk Industrial Park
York Road, Thirsk
N. Yorkshire, YO7 3BX
Telephone: 0845 524880

USA
Madeira Marketing Limited
600 East 9th Street
Michigan City
IN 46360
Telephone: 219 873 1000

AUSTRALIA
Penguin Threads Pty Limited
25-27 Izett Street
Prahran
Victoria 3181
Telephone: 03529 4400